The Pocket Business Coach

Creating and Enjoying an Entrepreneurial Life

Tim Mittan

Kendall Hunt
publishing company

Kendall Hunt
publishing company

www.kendallhunt.com
Send all inquiries to:
4050 Westmark Drive
Dubuque, IA 52004-1840

ISBN 978-1-4652-6035-2

Printed in the United States of America

Table of Contents

Introduction

I am a business coach. My job is to help my clients beat the odds. About 85% of new businesses fail within the first 3 years, and I want to make sure at least 85% of my clients succeed. The *Pocket Business Coach* is about how to make that success happen. But it is not all about the dollars and cents. The big picture never shows up on a balance statement, and that is both why so many of my clients beat the odds and why this book is different from other books on entrepreneurship. The secret is remembering that an entrepreneur is also a person. I don't mean that other business coaches assume they are working with squirrels or monkeys, even if the occasional excited entrepreneur might seem that way. I mean that in business coaching, in entrepreneurship, in life, we fail when we don't consider the whole person. I am not offering generic, one-size-fits-all formulas. My point is that entrepreneurs are different and have lives that need to be considered. Single or married, parenting or childless, gay or straight, hands-on or theoretical, risk-tolerant or risk-adverse—all of these aspects of the individual person matter enormously, not just in starting a business, but in being happy running one. Have you really succeeded if your business is thriving but your relationships, your health, and your sanity are all failing?

When I started coaching I truly believed I was only going to be answering questions about business. However entrepreneurs see business life and personal life as one. When one side has issues it bleeds over into the other side. Personal issues tend to be far more prevalent in the start-up phase. The bumps in their lives are usually due to the pursuit of their entrepreneurial dreams. However, with the correct coaching, entrepreneurs can navigate the bumps and continue on the road to success.

The Pocket Business Coach was not designed to be a story that is read from beginning to end that will give entrepreneurs the step-by-step process of starting a business. It does, however, provide insight into some of the personal journeys entrepreneurs sometimes take, along with business success strategies. Chapters can be read independently depending on the content need of the reader.

Foreword

The Human Side of Coaching

Why am I, a business coach, fielding all of these marriage-counseling questions? Why am I spending half of my time talking about relationships instead of the bottom line? These are the questions that led me to write this book. But considering relationships is only a small part of the book. What really matters is the larger idea of considering the entrepreneur as a complete and complex person, not just as one facet of a business. Doing that can not only help you start a thriving business while maintaining solid personal relationships, it can also help you run your business more profitably and more happily.

I know the basics of business from teaching business courses and from my own experiences running a business. I figured I would to have to learn more about business structures and tax incentives. I thought clients were going to ask me questions like how to get a Tax ID and how to file taxes. Standard questions like that. I knew my limitations and what I could and could not answer. I figured I would have to have an arsenal of lawyers, accountants, and marketers available in order to help me address some questions.

What I was not prepared for were the other questions, the personal questions. What I did not expect is that when one of these entrepreneurs likes and trust you, he or she comes to you for *everything*. I guess I was pretty shocked when I had an entrepreneur in my office who was very passionate about what he was doing and then began to cry. I did not really know why he was crying. He was just so happy that he had actually found somebody who would listen to him, and not just listen to him, but believe in him. He had found someone who could tell him that yes, he could be successful.

As a business coach it is awesome to see that passion in someone's eyes. They come alive whenever they get excited and start talking about their idea. You see that they want to actually do something for themselves. You see the creativity start to flow when they are talking about their craft or their skill or their lifelong dream. Then when you give them the tools to turn that dream into reality and say that you are willing to help them, you can see their passion and confidence grow. It is amazing, absolutely amazing.

Another component about coaching that I love is helping realize the ideas that entrepreneurs bring to me. It is encouraging to see when clients' ideas work and flourish. At that point I get to tell them how proud I am of their accomplishments. Many entrepreneurs do not have cheerleaders. They do not have people in their corners who are saying, "Hey, that's great! You did it!" Sometimes their customers do. Sometimes their spouses, life partners, or business partners will be their cheering section, but many times entrepreneurs feel they are in the effort alone. Whenever somebody who has watched them or is helping them tells them that they are doing well, that in and of itself is a huge boost to them because they do not get to hear it as often as they should. The pride I show in my entrepreneurs is genuine and they know it. They can see through B.S. in a heartbeat.

A Psychologist Entrepreneur

I first met Tim when he and my children were involved in a local theater production. He was passionate, resolute, and talented. I then had occasion to be a guest speaker for Tim in my role as a local entrepreneur and I saw him bring these same traits to his role as the Director of the Entrepreneur Center. I have had the good fortunate to launch three businesses during my career as an organizational consultant and mental health therapist and can relate all well to Tim's thesis that the entrepreneurial journey is an emotional journey and the coach's role expands far beyond business concepts and feasibility studies. I always felt that my business interests were like my third child in that I needed to show up every day with emotional clarity, a solid support system, and an abundance of love. Tim gets that. He understands that a human being sits across from him as he begins the coaching process and he not only asks but demands that the entrepreneur examines that humanity. If you read this book and incorporate the professional wisdom included, you will learn a few things about work. If you read this book and, as Tim would have you do, examine how your humanity intersects with your entrepreneurial spirit, you will learn a whole lot about you.

Sue Outson, MA, LMHP
Partner, Lincoln Wellness Group

Acknowledgements

I want to express my deepest gratitude to everyone who helped and supported and enlightened me during the writing of *Pocket Business Coach: Creating and Enjoying an Entrepreneurial Life*. Without all of you, I would not have been able to complete it.

I want to say thank you to my friends and family for their support. I especially want to thank Brooke, Linda, Cat, Terri, and Andy. When I said that I wanted to write a book, they were instantly behind me with encouragement along the way. I want to give a special thanks to Jennifer Overcamp, without whom the Pocket Business Coach would be nothing but thoughts compiled in text. She helped me navigate the pockets of chaos in my writing journey.

My biggest thank you goes out to the entrepreneurs at the Southeast Community College Entrepreneurship Center Incubator whose participation in business coaching led to the inspiration for this book. I am glad I could be a part of the accomplishments and challenges they encountered during their entrepreneurial journey. Not a day would go by when the same challenges were brought to my attention. Every day was something new. That is why I loved working with them all.

Finally, I would like to dedicate this book to my Mom, Phyllis Johnson, whose love, support, and business savvy helped make me who I am today. She gave me the freedom to explore new and exciting things but directed me when she knew what was best. Love you Mom, miss you much.

Chapter 1

Entrepreneurs: Who Are These People Who Risk so Much and Work so Hard?

When someone says they want to be an entrepreneur, I ask them why they want to be in business for themselves. I usually receive varied answers. Some tell me it is something they have always dreamed of, others say they know they can do it, and others are doing it because their current work situation is hellish. I believe it is important to tell them that if they do not have the deep-seated yearning in their heart, within their soul, to do this, then they may never be able to do it. Some people can do it and some people cannot. If they find they are a person who cannot take the risk, that is fine. They should not be discouraged because entrepreneurs need people who will work hard and who understand the entrepreneurial spirit. In today's business world, it is essential for a nonentrepreneur to understand how an entrepreneur thinks. If people understand who they are working for, this will improve their experience with the company and help the business grow and prosper.

When entrepreneurs come to me who do have the special something, that passion inside of them, I know they will do everything they can to succeed. They will just need a little guidance. My job is to figure out if what they need is a little coaching, a boost in education, or just moral support. They should always be willing to learn more about their craft, their industry, and their own business abilities.

Entrepreneurs have this feeling inside of them that they have to make a way for themselves. They have to create something that is brand new, or reengineer a product that currently exists, and run with it. They can take what somebody has already created and make it better. They also want to take a good idea, move it forward, and take their lives to a whole different place. Now if they are the type of people who need to know where their next paycheck is coming from, then they might not be able to be an entrepreneur. However, if they know they can eventually make money, and although it might take a little while, they can figure out a way to survive in the meantime.

Entrepreneurs have to be willing to take risks, but they should not show risk tolerance by doing stupid things. They need to take calculated risks. They have to understand what the pitfalls may be in what they are doing. To take a calculated risk, entrepreneurs will have to do the necessary research. That research, combined with their natural instincts, allows them to proceed with their plans. They can try a few things to see what works and then run with what does. They have to be able to get past the fear to make it work. If they can do that, they can make anything happen. That is what makes them so wonderful to be around; they have that drive and instinct, which motivates them to move forward.

Entrepreneurs tend to look at failure as not being the worst thing in the world that can happen to them. They learn from failure. It is not a bad word to them. It is just one of those things that can happen when starting a business. They say, "Well, that did not work. Now how do I make it better?" I am not saying failure isn't a bitter pill for them to swallow, but they get over it easier than most. They usually see a failure more as wasted time, not necessarily wasted money. Entrepreneurs should always be learning from these mistakes and should always be moving forward. In the entrepreneurship world, we tend to look at failure completely differently. It is actually a good thing to fail from time to time because that leads to learning. Adam Osborne, creator of the first commercially available portable computer, said, "The most valuable thing you can make is a mistake—you can't learn anything from being perfect."

Riding the Entrepreneurial Roller Coaster

I have worked with entrepreneurs when they have hit some very low points. They get discouraged. They do not understand why things are not working for them. They try to reach their target market in so many different ways, yet they are not making any money. They may bring in some cash for a short period of time, but it is not continuous. They get down. Most of the entrepreneurs I have worked with get depressed at one time or another; however, there is always this glimmer in their eyes. I can see the passion in their eyes because they want to succeed. They are willing to keep going. They just need a little encouragement. The low points usually stem from an idea that did not work or a slowdown in sales. An outsider's view of what is going on generally is all it will take to get them back on their feet.

As a business coach, I can usually spot a problem they are overlooking or think of a new marketing strategy or provide a resource they need. I see optimism in them even when they are down. I tell them that it does not hurt to take a break from time to time. This will sometimes bring them clarity on their issue. It is okay to be down. They need to have emotional downtime to go up and be positive. They are never going to be 100% on top of the game. They should always know that, but never lose their optimism. Optimism sustains entrepreneurs. It is what will keep them going. Entrepreneurs also have the desire to make it work. Whatever "it" is, they want to make "it" work. They are willing to put in the hours to do it.

Now if there is anybody out there who thinks that becoming a millionaire is the first thing, you need to think about when you become an entrepreneur and then they are sadly mistaken. Not one entrepreneur I know has had that as a goal in their business. There are very few entrepreneurs who will tell you that the whole reason they went into business for themselves was to become a millionaire or to make a lot of money. It is just not feasible. The ones who we see making a lot of money today usually struggled to get started. We only see the reward for all of their initial hard work. That is because entrepreneurial ventures in the beginning very rarely produce profit. The whole point of being an entrepreneur is to be able to go off and do something on your own. The number one reason that businesses fail these days is because of a bad management. It has little to do with lack of funding. It has little to do with a downturn in the economy. It is because people do not know how to run a business. That is why they fail. Entrepreneurs must strive to learn the art of business. They must work to make their management decisions better. They must work to make their businesses grow.

Many times clients come to me looking exhausted. I ask them when the last time they had a day off was. Jokingly, they reply, "Ha, ha. What's a day off?" They often are on the path to working themselves to death. Entrepreneurs have to remember to take time off. They have to take a break and get away. I understand they believe it is all about the almighty dollar. I understand about making money and keeping clients happy, but taking an evening off to spend with family, work on a hobby, play a round of golf, or sit in the backyard reading help to re-energize. They need that time to regain their strength, be it mental or physical. The dark side to entrepreneurs is that they tend to work way too much. They feel the need or obligation to keep going. Instead they need to learn how to create systems. They have to learn how to prioritize and all those other fun business terminology things that they learned in introduction to business classes or by reading business books. Entrepreneurs need to learn time management because they need time away from the business to help the business grow.

Are you the stuff entrepreneurs are made of? Here are some questions to consider:

- Do you bounce back from disappointment? Or does discouragement usually make you decide to pursue something else?
- Are you reasonably optimistic?
- Do you have a business idea that won't go away or a passion you want to do full-time?
- Or are you just ready to grab onto anything because you want a change or don't like your job?
- Do you enjoy learning? Think about the books, TV shows, and hobbies that you prefer—do they involve learning and challenges or just passive entertainment?
- What do you do when you are afraid? Do you freeze up or panic, or can you manage fear?

- Are you willing and able to ask for help when you need it?
- Can you admit when you've made mistakes?
- Are you adaptable, or do you cling to a plan of action even when it isn't working because it's your plan?
- Are you willing to work hard when you may not see results for a long time?
- What sacrifices are you willing to make and when are the sacrifices too much?
- And finally, the most important question of all: How badly do you want this?

If you find you aren't necessarily entrepreneurial material, that doesn't mean *never* start your own business. It might just mean *not now*. Many of the important qualities can be deliberately cultivated, and since determination, optimism, flexibility, etc. will also make you a better, happier, more useful person, what have you got to lose?

Entrepreneurs Are Real Characters

One characteristic I love about entrepreneurs is their dedication to hard work. They actually want to work. They are not afraid of hard work because they want to succeed. They will do whatever they have to do to accomplish their goals. Another characteristic of entrepreneurs that I have discovered is that they appreciate honesty and some even prefer brutal honesty. They really want an outside opinion about what they are doing. They need somebody to tell them the truth about their idea or the direction they want to take with their business. As a business coach, it is never our job to say, "What you are doing is wrong," but we can say, "You may be going down a wrong path," and then recommend alternate routes for them.

A characteristic of a more experienced entrepreneur is honesty with themselves. When I say honesty, I do not mean being down on themselves. Entrepreneurs do tend to see the bad side of situations. They find it very difficult to take a compliment. This is where as a coach I step in and show the positive in the experiences. I believe this is essential. As an entrepreneur, they need to look in the mirror and say, "I'm proud of what I am doing." I know that may sound corny, but if you cannot look at yourself in the mirror and say, "I am *very* proud of what I am accomplishing," who else is going to do that? Who else is going to stand there and tell you that? Try it. Better yet, do it.

Some entrepreneurs have spouses or life partners who will accept everything that they do. Some have business partners, family members, and friends who will stand behind them, but some do not. If they do not have anybody in their life, who will say "I am proud of you," then they may have to do it themselves. *That* is brutal honesty. If they can honestly take a step back, take a look at what they have created, and say, "I'm happy and I'm proud of that," then good for them. That is the mark of a strong and confident person.

Chapter 2

But Art Is More Fun than Accounting!

I love working with creative people. Someone who can build something out of practically nothing, who can turn a blank computer screen into a video game or cover a bare wall with a vivid mural—these people inspire me. However, as much fun as they are, what happens when their creativity outstrips their business sense?

In one case, I worked with an artist who not only created art but also collected it. He wanted to have a business where he could sell his own creations as well as what he had purchased. He also wanted to open a gallery for other artists who hoped to make money off of the pieces that they had created but did not want to bother with the business end of selling their own work. Knowing all of this, I began to work with him on opening his business. It was fun to see his intensely creative side, especially since he could make something out of scraps. A can of spray paint, some wood, and a little time mixed with his talent and voila—a beautiful piece of artwork!

What I found out, although, was that when creative people get bored, the creative side pushes aside practicality. My client received some funding from a family friend to get his business open. I suddenly discovered that he was taking the money and buying art supplies as well as buying pieces to put into the gallery. What I could not make him realize was that without the gallery he had no way of selling those pieces. I could not get it through his head that he had to continually work on the gallery to get it open and available to the buying public to sell his art and make money. I could never seem to get the "making money" part into his head. I tried to explain in several different ways that getting the gallery open was crucial even if it did seem boring to him. Even his friends tried to encourage him to focus on the business first.

When he did focus on the business, he would put all of his effort into the work. He found a location and even did his homework by evaluating the other businesses in the area. He knew he wanted his gallery to be a destination, so being located near other gallery-type businesses was essential. He would diligently work on the space to make it meet his standards. He created flow patterns on the floor and designated gallery spaces for other artists. He was about two weeks from what he had marketed as his grand opening date and still did not have all of the walls painted. I discovered that when he was painting the walls, it inspired him to go off and create something to hang on the walls that he had just painted instead of painting the rest of the gallery.

Knowing he was not going to get the gallery ready in time, we postponed the grand opening and created a plan that we both agreed was achievable. To make this an exciting experience, he decided that the work schedule should be by type of task not by time. This allowed time for creativity and for keeping him on schedule for his grand opening. Knowing that he needed a creative outlet from time to time, we set up a rule that once he had one entire wall completed, which included painting the wall and installing appropriate lighting, then he could create something that would go on that wall. This plan worked. We found a way for him to create and prepare his business for opening. With this new plan, he was able to get his business open within our set time frame and have a grand opening just in time for the holidays. Trying to get the creative types to focus on business can be an issue, but when they do, the businesses that they can create can be phenomenal.

Sometimes the creativity will take over and the business component just does not materialize for some artistic types. One client I worked with only for a few short months was Marcus, a musician. He was very talented. He played the guitar and sang. He could play almost any genre of music and could write a song on the spot. His dream was to start a recording business for unknown talent who had a difficult time booking a studio to create a demo that could be sent to record producers. Marcus knew there was a need for this type of business because he was his own target market.

Working with Marcus was an inspiration because he was so passionate about music. He told me that when he was in a creative mood, he could literally picture the notes in his head for the song he was writing. Once he had musical notes on paper, the words would just flow. I made the assumption that because he was so passionate about music, and could picture the type of business he wanted to start, he would be motivated throughout the steps to launching his business. I was wrong.

For Marcus, the ability to focus on the basics of starting a business was difficult. He did not want to take the time away from his music to concentrate on "inconsequential things" like applying for a Tax ID number, opening a bank account, or figuring out the marketing strategies for his upcoming gigs. He wanted to jump right to the part where he helped his fellow musicians and made money. He would spend his nights playing guitars with friends and talking up his new business, but then he would sleep all day and skip meetings scheduled with potential investors.

The time came for Marcus and me to sit down and have a frank discussion about his business potential. He said that he thought of having a business was, as he put it, sexy, but going through the process of building it was a drag. We discussed options like bringing on a partner who knew the music industry, but had a mind for business and could run the operations. He did not know anyone whom he could trust. We came to the conclusion that he should concentrate on performing. He knew how to get gigs and could draw a crowd when he performed. If he could land more stage time, he could meet more musicians and could potentially find a partner who could help him realize his dream. The last I knew Marcus was still a solo act and struggling to book gigs, but was very happy being a working musician.

When you are an artist, sometimes it takes more work to get through the icky stuff of business development to fulfill your dream. However, passionate artists find it richly rewarding when others are excited enough about what they create that they can build a successful business doing what they truly love.

Chapter 3

Work–Life Balance: Because Insanity Is Overrated

As I work with clients and help them either start or take their businesses to a new level, I ask personal questions. One of the questions I ask is how much sleep they are getting. I want to know that they are actually letting their minds rest. Entrepreneurs cannot work 20 hours a day and function correctly. They will start to make mistakes and have impaired judgment. They have to take time away from their business. I want them to devote time to their families, be it husbands, wives, partners, children, parents, or siblings. I want to make sure that they are sleeping, eating, and exercising. Their work–life balance tends to get out of kilter when entrepreneurs start a business or bring in a new product or service. When this work–life balance gets out of balance, the problems begin. Both families and employees feel it.

Entrepreneurs are sometimes so focused on bringing in revenue, they forget about everything else. From the very beginning when working with clients, I want them to understand that I know they want their businesses to succeed, but there also has to be time away from that business for it to stay fresh in their heads. We need to make sure that everybody involved in the business start-up process is functioning at full capacity. Time away is a wonderful way to regenerate the passion and productivity. Vacations are a very good thing and are usually one of the first things that are forgotten when people start businesses.

When Kari first came to me, I did not think she needed me. She is a professional trainer and had previously been in business for about 15 years although always in a partnership with one or two other people. In that time, she had been quite successful. When she came to me saying that she was breaking off from the group and going out on her own, I really did not see how I would benefit her. I assumed she had figured out everything that she needed to know and was doing fine if she had been in business for 15 years. Although begrudgingly, I went ahead and took her on as a client. I quickly found that she did well in a business with somebody else as the business-oriented person in their partnership.

Keeping organized was particularly hard for Kari because she had too much on her plate. When I talked to her about the business, she would tell me she was up until eleven o'clock at night doing "stuff." When I asked what "stuff" she was doing, I would hear about her family, the neighborhood association, and issues in her husband's business. Then I would hear about her house, and then more about her daughter, and even more about her family, but very little about her business. Then when we would talk about getting workshops and seminars put together that she wanted for her clients she said she had a difficult time getting people to sign up. What I found was that she was not getting marketing out until right before the sessions were going to start. She was not adequately preparing for her workshops. She was leaving correspondence with her clients to the last minute and did not give them enough time to register. I recommended that her marketing materials have concise and exact information, but they did not turn out that way. Marketing is all about the content and the ability to reach the target. She is a prolific writer and loves to tell stories. That talent works beautifully in preparing and delivering her workshops, but not so much in marketing. She would create a postcard to send out that was filled from top to bottom with the description of the workshop, not just a teaser sentence and a catchy title. The contact information, date, and cost were often lost in the script.

I tried hard to figure out the best way to work with her because she always seemed so busy with family obligations. Then one day she asked, "Why can't I get anything to work for me? Why is my business not growing?" At the time I was in a hurry, so my answer was quite blunt. I asked, "Do you want the truth or do you want me to gloss over the issue?" She said, "The truth, of course." I said, "Because you are trying to be a Mom, Wife, and Entrepreneur all at the same time. Every time I talk to you tell me in no uncertain terms that you feel like you are failing at all of the above. I don't know where you got the idea that being an entrepreneur was more important than being with your family. There is no way to do it all at the same time. You do have the ability to be a success at all three. However, you have to understand that, at times your business will take you away from your family and vice versa."

It was as though a huge weight lifted off of her shoulders when I told her that it was okay to have a smaller yet significant business so she could be a mom and do all of the "mom stuff" that she wanted without the guilt. She soon figured out that she could actually work with her clients while school was in session. And if she focused on the right clients for the right periods during the day, she could make decent revenue that could help support her family. She also figured out that workshops and learning sessions were a pretty tough gig to do all alone, so instead she started marketing herself as a public speaker in her given area. She could schedule her public speaking around her daughter's school activities. I could tell she was on her way to becoming that stable entrepreneur she seemed to rely on in her previous venture.

Before, there was no flow to her business because she was trying to cram too many tasks into a five-hour day and then do more activities when her daughter and husband were asleep. That is not how to run a family or a business. I had to let her know it was ok to be a part of her family and that she did not have to give up being a mother just because she wanted to have her own business. Her daughter will graduate from high school soon. We are working on a plan for her to grow her business when she sees more time in her schedule. She has clearly defined her business as working one-on-one with clients, accepting public speaking offers, and conducting corporate wellness seminars. She has been able to create a work–life balance that fits well with her family values.

Entrepreneurs tend to take on the world. They believe they have to do everything! Often I find that attitude from women entrepreneurs. They feel they have to be everything to everyone. Sometimes I have to tell them it is okay if they aren't all that. It was refreshing to see the change in Kari after this revelation. She was not stressing about much of anything anymore. She did not leave my office in tears anymore. She laughed, had a good time, and could even joke around. Being able to make this transition will make her an even better entrepreneur.

Frazzled Isn't Fun

When entrepreneurs do try to take on the world, they find in the beginning that they can juggle all of the tasks and keep up with the demands of the clients. They can usually do all of this because of the excitement that is generated from launching the business and going out on their own. They have the ability to juggle everything due to an adrenaline rush created by the risk associated with being an entrepreneur. They have their sights set on success and believe they can do whatever is necessary to succeed. However, what they do not anticipate is the client load becoming increasingly more demanding, too many tasks to juggle, and the amount of hours required to complete those tasks begins to take up precious time that most people would use for eating and sleeping. Entrepreneurs reach a breaking point when they have to ask, "How can I keep going at this pace?"

The question was recently asked to me by a client I had been working with for almost a year. She was working close to 20 hours a day at times, never saw her family, hadn't cooked at home in forever, and was stressed to the max. She was exhausted! She has two kids at home and a husband working on his PhD who was a grad assistant so therefore not really bringing in any money. He had a stipend, and most of it was going back into his college work, so she was taking care of the entire household and on top of it all was trying to grow a business. I could see pain in her eyes and in her posture. She was slumped over and could barely form sentences when she spoke. She had the weight of the world on her shoulders.

In her mind, she had to continue at this pace to provide for her family. She is a print specialist and knew that one more batch of business cards, one more new poster, or one more graphic design for a website was income for her and her family. I simply asked her why she had not taken a day off. She needed a day off. She needed to relax and unwind a bit. She got a bit ruffled and told me that her family needed her to work. I told her that she was wrong. Her family needed her at home and sane. I explained that if she could take eight hours of a weekend to spend with her family she could become rejuvenated. She also would be able to do so much more for her business if she actually relaxed and got a good night's sleep.

She didn't have any response for me. All she could think of at that time were invoices going out, work completed, and money coming in. I pushed the issue. In no uncertain terms, I told her that in order for her business to be any good at all or to grow, she had to figure out a way to get out of the office from time to time while still bringing in an income. That was the only way that she was going to be happy. She took the talk to heart. The first thing she did was hire her 21-year old son. It's kind of ingenious because the money is in full circle then. The money that comes into the business is paid to the employee who brings it back into the family. The son gets a paycheck but has to pay rent to live at home. The fun part about that is that the family dynamic is quite interesting. He wants to be just like her which means that he is very creative and wants to do all the fun stuff, but what she really needs him to do is all of the filing, answering the telephone (not making sales, just answering the phone), ensuring that the orders are completed, and getting them shipped out. She eventually wants him to work with customers, which means training. It will be interesting to see whether she can train him not in a motherly fashion but as an employee. She has to be an employer while at work then become a mom after work.

Hiring her son has proven beneficial in two ways. She has someone in the office to help her on projects, and she is able to see what she really needs in an employee. This information has helped her put together an employee jobs list and a potential job description. However, the biggest benefit to having someone else in the office is that she figured out what she thought she needed in an employee was a bit off. She learned that she didn't really need another design or creative person; she needed an operations person, someone who could come in and run the place.

She has hired a second employee and is getting ready for a third, and it's all based off of putting together the processes of the business, making sure the same thing is done the same way every time. She ran her business by herself for so long, but had never got the processes out of her head and on paper in order for them to make sense to anybody but her. This has been a valuable lesson for her which has allowed her to propel her business forward. It's fun to watch her growth because she has gone from being a frazzled individual whose goal was to be a breadwinner to someone who actually is thinking about business processes and how she can get more help to make her life easier and spend some time at home.

So You Want to Take a Vacation

As in hiring employees, to take time off, business owners must have systems in place so it is clear how the business operates on a day to day basis. Whether they are going to be the sole owner and work in the business forever or whether they intend to have a fleet of employees, it does not matter; they have to have systems. They have to layout how every component of their business operates every single day. All day-to-day activities, including but not limited to sales tactics, order fulfillment, and customer service have to be done the same way every time. These systems will save the entrepreneur if they go to hire somebody. When the system is written down and not just in their heads, they can show the new employee how something is done. They can walk away and then all they have to do is quality and control. If they are the only worker in the business from here until the end of time, the system can save them if they ever have a customer dispute or an issue with one of their clients. The entrepreneur can come back and say, "This is how I work; this is how I do it for every client." Systems are essential in creating a logical order in the business.

Chapter 4

Goals and Guts

"Am I doing the right thing?" This question is usually about the type of business new clients have opened, the product or service they sell, or just about being an entrepreneur in general. I always ask, "Compared to what?" Some seem to always want to go by society's norms on steady jobs, regular paychecks, and benefits. Then I ask, "Are you happy being an entrepreneur?" They usually say they are tired, but they are happy. I believe that as long as they are happy, they are at the starting point for creating something beneficial for themselves and those around them. If you wonder if you are doing the right thing, ask yourself: Am I happy? If the answer is yes, that means you are probably passionate about the business you are creating. It doesn't mean rich, it means happy. If you are happy, you are more than willing to put in more effort. That, to me, says more than anything that you are doing the right thing.

One serious issue regarding starting and growing a business is that entrepreneurs must minimize their risk. The entrepreneur and I talk about what would happen if they were to lose everything. What would happen if their business failed and they had to move on to something else? One of my mantras when I work with entrepreneurs is: "Home, Health, and Family." Every decision that they make is going to affect their home, their health, and their family in some way. If they feel good about a business situation (and entrepreneurs have a pretty good gut), then it is probably good. The next business opportunity comes along; they do a gut check because it does not feel quite right. Then it is probably bad. I try to get that into their heads. There is a difference between being scared and not feeling good about the situation. Those are two very different things. Feeling scared means, yes, there is risk there, but all indications point to going forward with it. But not feeling good means that something is not right, and if something is not right, then don't go there. All decisions in business have to feel right in order for them to work.

On a number of occasions, I have had entrepreneurs come into my office and talk to me about troubled marriages and troubled relationships because the business decisions they are making are not sitting well with their partners. Business relationships would be one thing, but they want to talk about marriages, engagements, domestic partnerships, things like that. Sometimes domestic problems occur when entrepreneurs are very passionate about what they do and happen to be involved with somebody who does not understand what it is that they do or why they do it. Life partners sometimes cannot deal with the risk and only see the downside to the business, constantly worrying what will happen if the venture fails. When this subject surfaces, I try only to deal with the business side of the issue; I then refer them to a professional who is better equipped to handle this type of situation. It is difficult to transfer that gut feeling to someone who just does not have the entrepreneurial spirit.

Mapping the Entrepreneurial Mind

Business coaches are lucky because we get to look at businesses from an angle the entrepreneurs do not. We are outsiders looking in at what they are doing. It is true we are not in their business every day, but by looking at their income statements or balance sheets, listening to their stories, and watching their body language, we can usually tell how their business is doing.

One of the things that coaches get to do is teach entrepreneurs how to step back and look at the big picture. When they can see the business as a whole they can, hopefully, be brutally honest with themselves. They will be able to tell what direction their business is going, evaluate a new service or product line, or decide whether a new employee is doing well in his or her role. The goal is to get them see their own true potential as a business owner and to determine what they are capable of doing in the business as well as what they *will be* capable of doing. To do this they need to "mind map" personal assets to see their strengths and weakness, current business structures, and brainstorm for the future. The "mind map" should reveal where they need help or have a weakness, as well as identify what comes easy to them. The weak areas both personally and in the business are targets for growth. That is where they have to find more education, a mentor, or hire someone who can fill that role. They also "mind map" their products and services. They list everything they have the ability to sell. Just because they have the ability to create and sell something does not mean they should. In addition, if they have several products or services they want and can sell, the "mind map" will help determine which should be the main focus of their business and what should be offshoots, or services for a later development. Mind mapping has been extremely successful in educating my clients. It aids in system development and create a clearer path toward their goals. According to Mindmapping.com mind, mapping has the ability to:

- Increase productivity
- Enhance meetings
- Simplify request for proposals
- Overview knowledge management
- Optimize project management
- Improve collaboration and communication

Mind mapping can be done formally or informally. There are software programs, online services, and professionals who will help you mind map for a fee. However, the best way to mind map is to break out the old markers and butcher paper and create it and keep it. Mind mapping is best done with one person who is familiar with the company, but not in the company. This provides an outsider's perspective that is necessary to get the entrepreneur to think outside of their business.

Goals Are Not Just for Sports

Often when I work with entrepreneurs, I receive basic questions and comments regarding starting or growing their businesses, such as how to secure a tax ID number. Other questions tend to require a little digging. When new entrepreneurs come into my office and say, "I need funding for my business," rarely are they ever at a point where they need funding. They are often at the "idea" stage. They more than likely do not have a business plan written, not that it is completely necessary for funding these days. So when somebody asks that question about funding, I know that is just the beginning of the conversation. The questions asked are often 10 steps ahead of where they really are in their start-up or growth stage. But that is just where they happen to be in their mind so they ask. My job as a coach is to find out exactly where they are and where they need to be. Once we discover exactly where the starting point is or we find out exactly where they are in their business, then we set goals.

Most entrepreneurs I have met are not big on goal setting. They want to go and do and become prosperous. They have innovative ideas they want to nurture and fun things to create. However, goals are the only way to get where you want to go. Goals create outcomes. Outcomes are measured. Measurable outcomes produce guidelines that help create revenue. Knowing the possible outcomes leads to creating marketing that helps to ensure entrepreneurs are on the right track. When I work with entrepreneurs, I want to make sure they have clear and attainable goals. Goals can be changed as the business progresses. One great thing about owning a business is being able to shift priorities to meet those goals any time they want. In the beginning, they just need to have something to aim for.

One of the best things to remember about being an entrepreneur is flexibility. They can restructure processes as their businesses grow. They can shift goals to create bigger outcomes. If a sales strategy is not working, they can adjust their revenue goal to something realistic based off previous performance. Although I often have clients work on financial goals like marketing and hitting a fiscal target, I usually suggest working on a personal goal as well.

The personal goal will generally be about education or research, but often I will have them include more time to be with their family and friends. Once I had a gentleman come to see me who had just purchased a restaurant. He complained that he never saw his children and wanted to get to a point with his business where he didn't have to be there as much and could be home with his three girls. It was a truly admirable goal. I was happy to work with him on it, even knowing that he was in the start-up phase of his restaurant which meant it was going to be at least three or four months before he was ever going to get to that point. I asked the age of his children. He looked at me very funny and asked, "Why?" I said I just wanted to know what age his girls were. He told me that they were between the ages of 8 and 14. Since it was legal in his state, I recommended that he have the girls work in the restaurant with him. Not cooking or handling knives or anything like that, but there was no reason why they could not help set tables during the down times. The older ones could be hostesses and seat people. They could work with the menu. He could teach them a little financial responsibility and have them take care of the cash register.

He had many options to include his children that would let them feel ownership in the business as well as spend time with their dad. It would feel like the restaurant was more of a family business rather than something Dad went off and did day and night so they never got to see him. In fact, he did take the two older girls to work with him and gave them duties they actually liked. For children to successfully join their parents working in the family business, it has to be something everyone wants to do. The children have enjoyed it and so has he. Eventually his daughters got busy with school and are not working down there as much, but at least they now understand what their dad was doing all the time and why he was gone so often. They also got to see his joy in running the business and how much it meant to him. Bringing the family together made them stronger and more understanding of the entrepreneurship process.

Goal setting is extremely important for the life of the entrepreneurs as well as for the life of their businesses. It helps them achieve that work–life balance. For example, I work with an accountant who has decided that he would like to spend more time being a father and husband. He is the owner of his business, but does not want to be working in his business constantly. He needs to pursue other opportunities that will help the business grow, such as more networking opportunities and social functions with his wife. When he is serving so many of the business's clients himself, he is not able to do that. He has two employees. Combined, these two employees do not bring in the amount of revenue that he does alone. Knowing this, he came up with the goal to be able to oversee the business, while being out and about networking for more business and also spending more time with his family. The latter was very important to him because he has small children at home.

The first question I asked him was, "How much money is it going to take?" Since he did not have that number off the top of his head, his first assignment was to find out how much money he needed to have coming in to meet that goal. Come to find out, the number was not nearly as high as he thought it would be. All he really had to do was double the current number of clients each of his employees was serving. This could be accomplished by creating a new marketing campaign and by joining additional networking groups. The numbers also lead him to the conclusion that by adding only one more employee, the number of clients could increase if he or she did networking and sales as well. He figured out that if he kept going at his current rate, he could achieve this goal in six months. Putting real numbers and real timetables to goals can help business owners see what their entrepreneurial ventures can become. It helps them get their mindset to a point where they can actually achieve these goals and then everyone can share in their success.

Is It Quitting Time?

A question that was quite difficult for me to answer as a coach was first posed to me a couple of years ago. I still get this question from time to time, although not very often. The question is, "When do I give up? When do I know that I'm not a success, and when do I start looking for a job? When can I quit?" It is kind of a shock to hear that because very rarely do entrepreneurs ever give up. They almost always look for alternate means to success. Or if one option doesn't work, then they go to the next one. That is what I expect from most entrepreneurs I work with.

When do I give up? was tough for me because I honestly did not know the answer. The question was posed a few years ago by Shane, an IT specialist who designed a website that could track stock trends. We talked about why he asked me that question. I needed to know what was going on. His most compelling answer was that he did not believe his business was making the impact in the market that he thought it should be making. He had a very hard time getting clients since some of his competitors provided the same information for free. He was new to the industry, so there was not a lot of knowledge about him or his company among his competitors, networking groups, or potential customers. He wanted to try to keep going, but he did not know that he could. He knew when he launched this business that it would be a difficult task.

My question back to him once I got a little bit of this background was, "So what job do you want to get?" That shocked him because I did not respond, "No, don't give up; you're better than that." I really wanted to know what kind of job he was looking for. He didn't have one in mind. I said, "Okay, if you're going to go for a job, let's talk about what kind of job you can get where you'll be happy." He gave me this puzzled look, like was I betraying him. A look of, *Why aren't you pushing me to be an entrepreneur, pushing me forward?*

The question posed was *When do I know when to give up?* In my mind, he had already given up by choosing those words. I wanted to push that a little bit more. So we talked about positions he would be qualified for and I started laying out his talents as I saw them. He was good at sales, he liked talking to people, and he had a definite talent in Internet technology. My solution was for him to try to find a young company, or new start-up, that would take him on as a sales rep. A position like this would give him the freedom to go and sell on his own without having to report to someone for long periods of time. He asked why I had suggested that kind of job. I told him it was because he told me that he would never be chained to a desk ever again. I told him we had to figure out a way to keep that from happening.

After I began laying out the perfect job for him, he realized I was describing everything he was supposed to be doing for his own company. Then I asked him why the sales approach we had designed, the new marketing, and the social networking components were not working for him. He did not have an answer. I asked point blank how long he had been working 100% on his own company. He answered, "A little less than a year." I said, "You thought you were going to perform miracles in a year?" He had extremely high expectations. He wanted to be supporting his business and his family in less than a year with a product that was difficult to sell, in a market that changed constantly.

Once he figured out where I was going with this conversation, we started talking about his sales goals, techniques he could use to improve his sales, marketing strategies based off of a feature/benefits model, and, most importantly, about his confidence level and the reality of his expectations. When we were finished I said, "When you start looking for jobs, you put me down as a reference. I would be happy to refer you to any company that would like to hire you." He said, "I won't go work for somebody else. I've been out on my own now for almost a year, and I love it. I just *can't* work for anybody else." I said, "So why are you giving up?" He said, "I'm not," and walked out of my office.

My challenge was to get him thinking about his company and his reality. That made all the difference. He figured out that anything he was going to do for any other company he could do for himself. He just had to do it harder, better, more often, and he had to set some realistic expectations. He had to set financial goals that were achievable so that he did not feel like a failure if he did not meet them. Shane had to realize that he had the ability to meet the goals that he set in front of him, and if he did not meet those goals, he had to do something that would change the outcome.

This was the correct direction for Shane. However, some entrepreneurs need to know when it really is time to give up. When I challenge an entrepreneur, I expect them to make the decision that works for them and their families. There are times when the business model they have created just will not work or the revenue that is generated will not meet the expenses of the business, let alone produce income for the household budget. It is at these times that honest conversations about the longevity of the business need to take place.

Now let's relate these ideas to *your* business or idea.

- Does your business plan make sense to you and others around you? Is it a service or product you can see a reasonable person wanting?
- Do you make decisions that other people think you should make but that don't match your gut instincts? What usually happens?
- What are your goals? How can you make them specific? For example, "I want to support my family" isn't helpful unless you know how much money that involves. Figure out the family finances, so you have a dollar amount to shoot for. Ditto for "I want to retire early" or "I want to travel for a year."
- What are your nonfinancial goals for your business?
- Are your goals compatible with your goals for your family life or relationships?
- Do you have goals or hopes for your family life and relationships? Are they written down?
- Are your goals compatible with sanity and good health?
- If you quit, what else would you do?
- If you keep going, is it reasonable to expect that eventually you will reach your goals? (Remember, it's not a simple binary of continue/quit, since you also have the option of adapting your business model to your current situation.)
- How can you help your family to be involved in or at least aware of what's happening in your business?

Chapter 5

Family Matters—But I'm Not Sure My Family Gets Me

I did not know that there were so many people out there who were dead set against family members and loved ones starting a business. It just blew my mind to find that attitude here, in this country, where we have the freedom to start a business on any given day if we so desire. Yes, there are hurdles, and yes there are risks. But we can start a business whenever we want.

So many people utterly oppose one of their loved ones actually going through this process. I met entrepreneurs who felt so alone because they were completely different from everybody else they knew. Nobody in their lives understood what starting a business or doing something on their own or something for themselves meant to them. It is crucial to them to have somebody to talk to who understands what they want to do, who agrees with them, and who not only embraces their idea, but is willing to help them take it a step further—to make it actually happen.

Once we get past the "What do you want to do?" questions, the next thing I ask is "What does your family, spouse, or life partner say about you going into business for yourself and what do they think about your idea?" Entrepreneurs are sometimes scared to talk to friends and family about what they want to do. Many times I will get the answer, "I haven't told anybody yet," or "Nobody knows," and I ask why. The answer tends to be "Because I don't know how they will react when I tell them." This leads me to believe that the spouse or partner does not have an entrepreneurial background and may not completely understand what it means to be an entrepreneur and the spirit that dwells inside someone who is. On the opposite end of the spectrum, I will get the response, "Yes, I have told them and they are not thrilled, but want me to look into it." That is usually why they are sitting in front of me, to get answers. That tells me that if the entrepreneur goes forward, there will be challenges at home, but the support will be there, especially when they share their first successes. On rare occasions, I get the answer, "Yes, my family knows and they are behind me. They even want to help once I get started." Those families get the concept of entrepreneurship or have some entrepreneurs in their lineage and are happy to support that spirit in the people they love.

When I talk to entrepreneurs, I am very honest about the fact that they can talk to me, another business coach or consultant, or anybody who understands their plight all they want, but at some point in time, we are going to go away. They have to figure out how to talk to their loved ones. It is better all around when they make that happen early on. Entrepreneurs have to talk to and get support from the people in their lives. If they are married, their spouses have to understand what starting a business is going to mean for each of them. They have to understand how it is going to affect their lives. They have to understand that the entrepreneurs' creativity and passion are going to take them away from the family from time to time. They have to understand that the business is going to become their entire life, at least for a little while. It is going to become the family's life.

Entrepreneurs tend to play their cards close to the vest, but if they trust someone, they will open up and show their entire hand and sometimes the rest of the deck. After working with entrepreneurs for a while, I can see the telltale signs of when they are beginning to open up. I look for those times when they are not being forthright with information. There is always a reason why they are not being completely truthful. It's not because they don't want to tell the story. It's not because they are afraid of failure. There has to be something behind withholding the information. I dig deeper, I probe with more questions. I try not to be personal, but normally if I can continue the conversation, the real problem will come out. I can usually find the "aha" moment in their answers. Once I have figured out the real reason for their questions, lack of contact, or hiding of information, we can work on a solution that will help them and their business.

In one such instance, John, who had been working with me for almost a year came to me out of the blue and told me that he had to rebrand his business, bring on a new line of products, and create a whole new website. This came as a complete surprise to me since we had worked very hard in establishing his current brand, product line, and website. He had just launched a major marketing campaign that would help him solicit more business. Now I am not a big fan of rebranding a business unless it is absolutely necessary. Rebranding should only be done after merging with another business, taking on a partner, or if the main mission of the business changes. There had to be a reason behind this new strategy.

After roughly a 30-minute conversation about why all of this was necessary, how much hassle it would be to change everything we had just created, and what the costs associated with all of these changes would be, the real story came out. Apparently John and his wife had had a fairly heated discussion about the finances after dinner the week before. John told me they started going through the family budget with a fine tooth comb. His wife said they were not making as much money as they had in the past when he had a full-time job and she was not happy about it. She didn't get the raise that they thought she was going to get. He had yet to earn steady revenue, and all the money that *was* coming in was only paying for business expenses. They had not contributed to the kids' college fund in over a year, the van was on its last legs, and they just found out their oldest needed braces. All of that combined was the reason for the big shift in his business model. He was feeling guilty for not providing for the family and was getting pressure from his wife to contribute the kind of money that he had before he was an entrepreneur. He believed that by rebranding himself and taking on a new product line, he would be able to venture into other markets and create more revenue more quickly.

Now that the real story was out in the open, we could come up with viable solutions to his problems. Rebranding was not going to help. However, we did talk about a new product line and some new marketing strategies. We also discussed how far he had come in his business and all of the prospects he had for contracts. He was on the verge of landing a substantial project that would last for several months. The revenue generated would more than cover all of the issues he had just talked about. I told him that he had to sit down and explain all of that to his wife so she, too, would understand the processes he was going through to make money. He agreed that he had not fully disclosed everything he was doing. At one point in the conversation, we even discussed the possibility of giving up his business and finding a full-time job with benefits and a retirement account. His response was immediate: He would hate it and would be a miserable person to live with. Knowing him and his personality, I wholeheartedly agreed. He did talk to his wife and smoothed things over at home, although effectively communicating is still sometimes a struggle for him.

Entrepreneurs sometimes struggle with the passion they have for being on their own and the responsibilities they have in their household. Guilt can play a very big role in the success or failure of a new business. Entrepreneurs and their families must be on the same page when it comes to starting a business. There may very well be hard times in the beginning, but when the success does come, every family member will benefit.

My Family Still Doesn't Get Me

I joke that 90% of what I talk about with clients is something other than the basics of business. The truth is I do not get just business questions from business owners, I get life questions. I am not a life coach, I am not a psychologist, but they trust me and consider me a confidant because I have been helping them get through something that they have really wanted to do all their lives. They trust me, so they talk to me about many things, including family. As always, I preach to them that every decision that entrepreneurs make will affect their homes, their health, and their families. I reinforce the idea that they have to do all they can to take calculated risks. They have to have that in their heads every time they make a decision. With the help of a coach, they can create a process to minimize the risk. Due diligence, a strong understanding of the industry, and confidence will always be necessary for this process.

I was scheduled to meet with a client who needed some basic information about starting a business. I figured he would want to know about obtaining a tax ID number, business planning, hiring employees, finding funding, or challenges like that. I was not prepared for the questions that were really plaguing him. When he told me he was scared to talk to his wife about his plans, my reaction was to avoid the personal questions and to tell him that he should be able to figure that out for himself. But when I looked into his eyes, I could tell he needed an honest answer. From that point forward, I have always tried my best to answer any and all questions that come my way except for ones that I am not qualified for.

This particular young entrepreneur came to talk to me about opening a gym. It was to be an athletic venue where patrons could do rappelling and Olympic-style training. He wanted to open it in the area of town where he and his family lived because he knew there was no such facility there. He loved that type of physical training and had managed a similar company earlier in his career prior to getting married and moving away for school. After he asked a few questions on how to open that type of business, and my thoughts on the best locations, he asked out of the blue, "How do I tell my wife what I want to do? She doesn't understand me. She believes I need to be working full time, but I really want to have my own business. I don't even know how to bring it up to her." I was speechless. I had no answer for him because I was only looking to provide business advice on his new venture. I ended up giving him some noncommittal remark about spouses being generally supportive, making sure he explained his plans carefully and thoroughly and to tell her about the potential. With that information, she should get on board with the idea.

I thought that would be the end of that conversation. However, about two weeks after the initial meeting, I received a phone call from him asking if he could come in and see me again with more questions. This time when he came in, he brought his wife. I assumed she was there to learn more about what he was doing. Instead, I quickly found out he wanted me to explain to her what he was doing and why it would be beneficial to them as a couple in the long run, and how he could go about it with my help and become a success. This was the first she was hearing of these plans. She was caught off guard and so was I. I found myself in a position I really didn't want to be in because I could tell immediately from the look in her eyes how upset she was at her husband and at me. I had not done anything that I knew of except support him, but I had also given him encouragement to go forward and look at something that could potentially, in her eyes, ruin their world. She had no problem expressing that to me, or telling me how upset she was that he wanted to ruin their world. I looked at him to see if I could find an easy way out, but he had this pleading look on his face for me to make it better. I tried to do just that.

I encouraged her to look at the venture from her husband's standpoint and how happy opening and running this type of business would make him. I asked her if she was confident that her husband had the ability to train people. She knew that he was good at that because he was doing it at his current job. Her main concern was not knowing how he was going to be able to start his own business in a town where they knew few people and make a success of it. They wanted a family, and she needed and wanted security. I started asking her a series of questions: What were her fears? Why did she not think that it would be successful? How did she see herself playing a role in the business? Then I went on to talk about financial rewards that can happen when a business succeeds. I also emphasized the freedom in his schedule that he would have once he was able to hire an additional trainer. I pointed out that he wouldn't be working as much on the weekends, which would give them more time together in the long run. I did state that it would be a struggle at first, but if she helped it would not seem so bad. I asked if she was working and had benefits. She was and did have benefits, but was not bringing in nearly as much as he was, and it would be a burden on the family if he just quit his job.

After an hour of talking, he was happy that everything was out on the table; she was a little less annoyed with the whole thing, but I could tell that she was not a happy person and she did not really want to be a part of it. Unfortunately, I don't always learn the outcome of my work with clients, and this was one of those cases. I do know that the business did not start, at least not where he said it was going to.

Hey, I Think My Family Is Starting to Get Me

Lots of entrepreneurs will ask me: "Will you talk to my wife?" "Will you talk to my husband?" "Will you talk to my girlfriend? They just do not understand what it is I'm trying to do." I have done that. I do not like doing it. I am not a trained mental health professional and I do not want to play marriage counselor. However, because I want to see them succeed, first I try to have them do it themselves. They have to find a way to actually talk to their spouse themselves and explain how it all works in a way that everybody will understand. I will do it only as a last ditch effort.

It is vital that family members stand behind their entrepreneur during the good and the bad. It is sometimes tough for them to grasp what is going on, especially if they are only accustomed to an eight-to-five job with a paycheck that comes in twice a month. Sometimes spouses will want to talk about what their husbands or wives are doing. I try to explain the process of being an entrepreneur to them and a little bit about how their minds work. In one such instance, a client brought his wife in to talk to me because she just did not understand what he wanted to do. When Vinnie (a long-term client) and Michelle came in, there was a definite tension between them. She was not happy and he seemed very agitated. After a short discussion of what Michelle knew about what Vinnie was doing, it was easy to see that Vinnie had not told her the complete story of the process he was going through in writing the business plan or what the long-term goals were for him and his family. It was also very clear that Michelle was a cut-and-dried, hard facts kind of person who wants everything in order.

I explained to Michelle the process of starting the kind of online business Vinnie was contemplating. He had conducted research, then he had performed a detailed industry analysis, and now he was in the process of writing his business plan. He was also trying to simultaneously create the website and order inventory, so he was prepared to launch just as soon as he had completed his marketing. Once I told her the story, she indicated that Vinnie had left out all of the research bits and jumped right into the part where he needed money for the website and inventory. He started in the middle of the story because that was where his mind was. I reminded Vinnie that just because he was in the middle of the story in his head didn't mean everyone around him had kept up with him and that they should be filled in on the entire story. I also reminded Michelle that she married a man with a passion to do something on his own. I assumed it was one of the attributes that she liked in him when they met. Now today they are working together to make the business a success. The plan is for Michelle to quit her job and join Vinnie as a partner in the business. She even has plans for her own venture one day, but that is another story.

Another issue that was brought to me at one point in the beginning of my coaching career that I had some difficulty with was: "My wife saw the end of year financial worksheets for the business and wants to know why the checkbook does not have the same amount in it as the income statement has in it." He had been talking to his wife about his business and up to this point she had been very supportive. She knew it was going to be a struggle when he launched and did everything she could to help out financially. He was good about keeping her up to date on how the business was progressing, but was still not really making any money. In hindsight, he should have stated that the company was making enough money to support itself, but there was not much extra. Almost every dollar left over was reinvested into the business and very little was coming to him in a paycheck. In the grand scheme of things, he had made approximately $10,000 that year, which for a beginning entrepreneur is pretty good.

When the income statement said $800,000 income and the checkbook over the year only said $10,000, she naturally wanted to know where the rest of the money had gone. He and I had a series of discussions about communicating clearly with his spouse and how to help her understand that all of the money that comes into the business does not go into the checkbook. He basically did a very short business course with her, showing her how the money that comes into the business is considered revenue and the revenue then has to be divided out into expenses and reinvested back into the business. What is left over at the end can then go home with the business owner. We also had to discuss how to do this without talking down to her. Thankfully, she understood everything and realized that he was making good choices about using the revenue to develop the business.

A few months later, I asked him during one of our sessions if he had told his wife how his business was doing because I knew he had had a substantial increase in revenue. He said he had not because of their new baby and her being exhausted all the time. I told him that he really needed to talk to her because he had just hired his first employee. Employees take a huge chunk out of the revenue stream. I let him know that he really needed to sit his wife down and tell her how these new expenses were going to work in his business so that he could prevent unnecessary stress in their relationship. He agreed. When last we spoke, he expressed that he was very excited to share with his wife the upside to a successful business. He now has three employees, his processes are in place, and he is bringing in more revenue than ever. He now has more time to spend with his new daughter, with a nice increase in the funds in their personal checkbook.

Chapter 6

In Order to Be Big Sometimes You Have to Start Small

When entrepreneurs begin to imagine themselves as business owners, they often jump from the idea stage directly to operating a full-scale business. They see all of the machines they need to purchase and the supplies or inventory needed on hand, as well as the large staff necessary to operate such an enterprise. This is often true of entrepreneurs who go through some sort of business training session where they have to write a business plan. Not that that is a bad thing, but for some, it tends to bring on an expectation that they must be at full operation the day they open the doors. Business planning is essential, but for some, it puts fear into their hearts rather than giving inspiration.

One such entrepreneur was Brad, who was in his mid-twenties with a wife, and a child on the way. When I met him, he had completed a 10-week entrepreneurship training series that provided him with the information necessary to start and operate his business. At the point of our meeting, he had been out of the sessions for almost six months. When I asked about the progress of his business, he indicated that he had not yet started. He had been unable to raise the capital necessary to launch his business, so he was working two jobs to save money while providing for his family.

He wanted to create a bicycle rental business which would keep his community green while providing transportation around the seaport city where he lived. The research conducted for his business plan indicated he needed about $100,000 to start his business. This amount would make sure he had enough capital to buy at least 30 bicycles, rent a facility for storage, purchase office equipment, and hire a manager to help run the company. He believed that he could only start his business on a large scale because it was the only way for it to be profitable.

I asked how many hours he worked at his part-time job. He said it was about 15 to 20 hours a week. I told him that I thought that time would be better spent working on his own business rather than for someone else. How much had he been able to save at his part-time job? He indicated that it was not nearly enough to launch his venture, but he had at least a couple thousand dollars. I then wanted to know if that was enough money to buy three or four bikes. He shrugged and said he thought so. I indicated that I was sure in his courses, he must have completed a feasibility study and the prospects must have looked good in order for him to continue pursuing this type of business. I then asked if he knew anyone who did not have much to do on the weekends and who would be willing to help him if he asked. Maybe some of his coworkers would like to make some extra money on the side. With a very quizzical look, Brad replied that he could think of some people like that. I could see he was ready for an explanation for all of my questions.

I told him that from the information he had provided, I thought he could launch his business and become successful prior to having the $100,000 indicated in his plan. If he bought four used bikes along with some spare tires and spare parts, he and his employees could start renting them out on the weekends. He could market the rentals in one or two of the local hotels that generally hosted tourists. He could sell maps of the area along with renting the bikes to make a little extra revenue. He could also speak to some of the restaurant owners along the bike paths to see whether they would give coupons or discounts of some sort to customers who came into their place of business and mentioned the bike owner's name. I could see the wheels start turning, figuratively, in his head. He was catching on to what I was saying. Once he began making revenue from the bike rentals, he could purchase more bicycles and begin to hire people to help run the operation during the week while he was at work. A business that currently has a revenue stream is much more attractive to investors and bankers. He would have assets for collateral if needed. He could even approach a specific bicycle manufacturer for a sponsorship.

If he started small and built the business, he would have the security of his full-time position while he created a revenue stream from the service he provided, and he would be able the test the rental model he had created on paper. It is a less risky to start small. The amount of money invested does not seem as big and if lost, would not be devastating to him or his family. He could also change the model as the business grew, if need be. Sometimes what we imagine in our heads or write down on a piece of paper seems like the best idea ever. However, once in play, it could look completely different. Sometimes starting small helps to perfect the business model while requiring less capital for the initial investment.

A similar situation happened with a photographer I was coaching. He had gone through an entrepreneurship training program that required writing a business plan. All of his research and studying was beneficial to him, as he had never thought much about the business side of owning a photography studio. He was an artist who took wonderful photos. He wanted to take that talent, become more mainstream, and create a business that could help sustain him and his wife.

Once he completed the program, though, he seemed a bit distraught. After a conversation about the information gained during his coursework, he said that he was not sure how he was ever going to get his studio off the ground. He was going to need several thousand dollars to fund the new equipment, computers, and backgrounds, and a building to house it all. I asked if he had a working camera. He laughed and said he did. I also asked if he preferred working indoors or out, if he had the ability to create photo albums digitally, and if he had access to a client base. All of his responses were yes. "Then," I asked, "Why are you not in business?" I indicated that he had all of the tools necessary to create income. He even had the one asset that made it possible for his business to be a spectacular success: the talent necessary to take stunning photos.

Sometimes the grand scale of business planning and dreaming can get in the way of creation. Entrepreneurs are designed to dream big and I would never want them to change that. What they have to remember is that what they perceive to be a starting point may not be. Sometimes if they scale back and refocus their vision, they can see that the starting point is within reach and what they had envisioned as their business is actually farther down the road. They can get there; it just may take a little more time than they thought. But when they do, it will be much better than they had envisioned and will potentially be all theirs without any liens to banks or investors. Sometimes you really do have to start small to grow big.

Chapter 7

Tools Not Found at a Hardware Store

Today's entrepreneur has to have several tools at hand to be successful. They need to use the appropriate tool at the appropriate time. They need to make sure they are taking calculated risks, and that nothing they are doing is going to harm their home, their health, or their family. To be successful, entrepreneurs really have to have a commitment to what they are doing. A lot of people want to start a business just because they think they are going to make piles of money, have a lot of free time, or they want to be the boss and just run the business without having to work. Any true entrepreneur will tell you that those can all happen, but should not be the expectation going in.

Knowledge

The first tool an entrepreneur should have is knowledge—knowledge about their skills, business sense, and finances. They also have to understand that there is a process for getting started. Many entrepreneurs do not have loads of money when they get going. Most are not born to money nor do they have hundreds of thousands of dollars stashed away to start this venture. Most have to do what is called bootstrap the start-up. Bootstrapping basically means to use all of one's own resources, financial and otherwise, to start a business venture. This can be a rewarding experience, both emotionally and financially. Bootstrapping means they must have a commitment to their idea. This commitment is imperative in order for them to succeed. They have to make sure that they are in it to win it, as they say. They have to make sure that they have support systems in place, and they have to continue to work and rework their ideas as much as necessary until they create a model that will lead them to success.

Business Sense

Another necessary tool is some business sense. I meet a lot of people who have talent or the ability to create. I meet people who are artists, people who can weld, people who are musicians, people who can write books, and accountants, just to name a few. However, to succeed in business, they first have to understand how business works. If they have not had a business class at all, they need to take one, read books about business, or learn from an expert. There are so many ways to get business knowledge in today's world. Most people who have worked for somebody else have a basic understanding of how businesses work. If they sit back and take a look at everything that happens on a day-to-day basis, they may start to see portions of the business they had never noticed before. Most people don't go in at eight, punch out at five, only do what is in their job description, and never notice anything going on around them. Anybody who has been at one business for a significant length of time will almost always know what was going on in almost the entire business. An entrepreneur—somebody who wants to step out of that nine-to-five world—needs to understand what they were doing, why they were doing it, and how they can take that knowledge with them.

In many cases, entrepreneurs learn how to conduct business by being employees at a company for several years then deciding to go out on their own. Let's take engineers, for example. In most cases, engineers have worked for other companies and have developed products, unique designs, or a distinctive process they can take with them when they leave. Legally this should be done with the consent of the parent company. This allows the engineer to contract back to the parent company at a higher rate than what the engineer would be paid, but at a lower cost to the company since they do not have to pay benefits. Often people who use the product become clients of the engineer when he leaves the parent company. Those clients will help him be successful. Any time entrepreneurs have an automatic revenue stream, and it helps them become a success more quickly. Most entrepreneurs do not have a business degree. Most have a degree or experience in their field of expertise. Therefore, the business component has to be learned. The desire to obtain that business education is key. It does not matter how they become educated. It does not matter if the class is credit or noncredit, a workshop at a conference, or something that they see on television, or participate in online. As long as they become educated in business, that is all that matters. That is one of the main tools necessary to becoming successful.

People on Speed Dial

There is another old saying that says in your back pocket you need to have a banker, a lawyer, a finance person, and an accountant who can help out at any given time. These people could be considered advisors to entrepreneurs. They have all been through the process of starting a business or they have helped people through that process. Knowing a banker, a finance person, an accountant, and a lawyer who are willing to give frank advice on a business endeavor can be crucial to success. If entrepreneurs do not know any of these professionals, they should try to make these connections as quickly as possible.

Mentors and Coaches

Another tool to add to the list is a business coach or someone to go to for business advice. Accountants, lawyers, and bankers all have great knowledge and experience, but most of it comes from their own industries. A business coach is someone who should understand all of those industries and be able to explain how they work as a whole for the entrepreneur. Business coaches give business advice but are not consultants. They are generally vested farther in the entrepreneur's life than just a casual one-time consultant. If a business coach is not available, then an entrepreneur should find any trusted person who has been in business for a long time. It is necessary to always have people who are cheerleaders in addition to the family, spouses, life partners, and friends.

I know it is not the most fun thing in the world, but planning for a business is extremely important. Think about the investment that is being made. I don't care if you are cleaning houses and all you need is a vacuum cleaner, a towel, and a couple of different cleansers. It does not matter how much money is being put into the business start-up. The thing is, at some point in time, there will be a lot of money and time invested so all the decisions made have to be well thought and good. The only way to make that happen, really, is to plan it.

Some see a business plan as some form of evil that makes people cringe whenever they hear these words uttered. Business planning is not always about sitting down and writing a 32-page paper on how your business is going to operate, the industry, target market, and everything else. Business planning can be very simple and can be done in a page. It is making the time to take whatever is rolling around in your head and putting it on paper. That helps provide an outline. It helps create a step-by-step process. It maps out the journey. It gives you the ability to see the business in writing and say, "Yes, I can do this." The most basic business planning should involve information about the company, the products or services, the industry, competition, the target market, some basic marketing and sales strategies, basic operations outline, and financial predictions.

Systems

Another tool that I truly believe in is the creation of systems. Entrepreneurs tend to think that they are their businesses and that that business would cease to exist without them. Unfortunately, they tend to always want to do *everything* in their business. In the start-up phase, that is not such a bad thing. They have to understand their books, marketing, sales, and production. Many times to understand all of it, they have to be involved in all of those functions. But as the business grows and they grow as a business owner, they have to know where their talent is best used. It could be working with the product or working with the clients. However, if they need someone to do the back office or the operations stuff, then they should hire someone. The hard part tends to be relinquishing control of any part of the business.

The best way to make that transition is by creating systems. Systems should be created for back office operations, inventory control, retail operations, and client relations, even answering the telephone or responding to emails. The entrepreneur has to understand exactly how the process works to write it down. They cannot have it rolling around in their heads and expect others to "just catch on." It has to be on paper somewhere so that when somebody new comes in to take over that task, they can read how it should be done. This allows every employee to run their portion of the company the same way. The owner's job becomes quality and control—making sure the employees are really doing their jobs as prescribed by the systems. They are now representing the company brand and work should be done in the best way possible. By creating a system early on, the entrepreneurs can step away sooner and let the business run without them.

This is important because at some point the owner will want to take a vacation or just an afternoon off. They need to have a break from their business. It does not matter whether it is a day or two or a week or two—they have to have time away. If they have a family emergency and have to be away or if they themselves become ill, the business needs to continue in their absence.

Marketing

The final tool that is extremely important is being able to understand the importance of marketing. Most people say, "I'm not good at marketing." Well, they just have to get over that. Promotion is a key component in running a successful business. Business owners do not have to be design wizards or have golden tongues to be good at marketing. They just have to know their target market and how that demographic receives information. One very simple form of promotion is putting a good face out in the community by participating in or sponsoring community events. Promotion is working with a marketer to come up with advertising that is good for your company. Promotion is also giving product away to a charity, to a raffle, or for fundraising in exchange for exposure. It is sponsoring the little league team in your town.

Marketing the business is huge, especially at start-up. The process of marketing and promotion begins even before the doors open. Start by telling the people you love—friends and family. They will help you to become a success. Once in business, never stop promoting. Everybody says that word of mouth is the best. It can be. I will not deny that. Word of mouth is a wonderful form of marketing and promotion. But word of mouth can be negative as well as positive. Never rely 100% on word-of-mouth marketing. Make sure to use several forms of marketing that speaks directly to the target market.

Planning, systems, promotion, having business sense, knowing or hiring a banker, a lawyer, an accountant, a coach or mentor, and most importantly the commitment to the project. All of these things combined will help any entrepreneur be a success.

Chapter 8

Are You a Want or a Need?

Just because economics seems boring, does not mean you can ignore it. (It actually won't seem that boring when you understand how it affects your bottom line. Read on…) So here's a thumbnail sketch of Economics 101 without all the irrelevant parts. Now I know that it's hard to figure out the health of our economy when the *Wall Street Journal* headline seems to be contradicted by the NBC news report because they are both citing different facts and sources. The broadcasters, special interest groups, and television figureheads are all telling us how to think and what to believe. Politicians are giving their take on the economic situation. If, heaven forbid, it is an election year, the real story about how the economy is doing is more than likely going be buried under political rhetoric.

A new business owner really needs to do his or her own research to find out what the economy is like. In most cases, whether the economy is up or down, there is never a bad time to start a business. If the economy is down, then the price for inventory or property may be at an all-time low. Take advantage of the lower costs and buy the supplies you need or purchase the storefront you desire. However, you may have to budget more for marketing to get customers through the door. Inventory may be a little bit cheaper because people are looking to sell or liquidate. Property can be purchased cheaper, and rent is lower—there are many positive things that can happen financially when the economy is slow. On the other hand, if the economy is good, it may cost more to get into the game, but people should be more willing to spend. This will help create an instant revenue stream from buying customers.

When evaluating the economy, look for the resources that are available such as information that is available on economic development websites, unbiased economic reports, and through your local economic development centers. This will take some research but will become a daily routine when you see the value in this information. Another way to find the information is to contact the local community college, small business development center, or entrepreneurship center. They should know all of the up-to-date economic forecasts, legislative bills regarding small business, and funding information. If the economy is bad like it was in 2008 and 2009, find out what the government is doing to help the small business owner. During such times, the government will often pass initiatives that will help with funding or provide tax incentives to help restart the economy.

When the economy starts to recover, it is also a good time to start a business. Even though inventory, property, and supplies might be a little more expensive, attracting customers will be easier. When the economy is in an "up" trend, clients are more in the mood to shop. They are willing to spend as opposed to saving for a rainy day. Prospective entrepreneurs must identify their target markets and learn what those potential customers' spending habits are and what exactly they are looking for. Those consumers need to be convinced that your new store offers the best quality product, along with the best service. More money is going to be spent on marketing, inventory, and, potentially, for property. However, the return will be faster because the customers with cash in their pockets will spend a little more readily.

There is something called elasticity of demand that is based on wants and needs. If the product being sold is elastic, that means it is a want and people can live without it if money becomes tight. If it is inelastic, it means that people usually need it to survive in some form or another and will cut other costs to purchase that product or service. Most people start businesses with products or services that are wants, and only rarely do we start businesses with a needed product.

Maslow's hierarchy of needs helps us understand what we need to survive. We need food, water, shelter, and clothing. Those are all of the basic needs. Everything else above that tends to be a want. Most lifestyle businesses provide services that we can live without. We have to make sure that when we create businesses in the *want* category, the customers are able to fulfill the want they currently think they need. If not, sometimes an artificial need is generated for the product or service, usually done through advertising and marketing. That is tough to do. It is difficult to always have your audience's attention. It can cost money to do this, especially at a time when people are not buying.

If consumer confidence starts to drop, and the economy starts to head south, the last thing that should be cut is the marketing budget. Unfortunately that is often the first thing business owners tend to do: cut their marketing budget at a time when they need it the most! Look at other ways of cutting back, such as eliminating unnecessary expenses or other nonessential costs. Small business owners have a tendency to be fiscally leaner and are able to make financial adjustments easier than larger corporations. Marketing is needed the most when the economy starts to turn, and when it dips a little bit, businesses need to make sure people see them more often. That is also when the customer service should ramp up. That is when the quality of the product or service has to be the best. Businesses must make sure that no matter what the economy is doing, their client wants them—and not only wants them, but believes that they need them.

Any type of service, even getting a haircut, can be a want because it really, truly can be done at home. I know, but don't laugh. It can be done at home. It can be done by somebody who is not a professional. Massages, going to movies, the theater, and a new bike are all wants. They can all go by the wayside when consumer confidence starts to fail.

People can do many things to save money when the dollar is tight. We saw it in the last recession. People stopped building homes. The homebuilders suffered; however, contractors who did repairs and remodeling did a booming business in that time because people stayed where they were. They decided to update what they had so they spent more money remodeling and renovating. They did not have to buy a new house. Even though one sector did not do well in that time frame, another sector did. If the housing trends were on their radar, contractors would have known to spend more money on marketing, being part of trade shows, and telling people they needed to update their current living space. Most contractors in 2010 were booked out over a year in advance because people wanted them to come in and re-do their homes. Understand and know the economy. It will definitely benefit you in the long run.

Chapter 9

Ready, Set, Go!

The Light Bulb Just Went On

The catalyst for starting a business varies from person to person. Some become entrepreneurs because of the spirit within, some find a niche, and some have a craft or skill they believe can make money. For this reason, the main component of these ventures, the idea, can span the spectrum from new technology to capitalizing on a hobby. When starting a business, many things need to be considered such as the economic health of the business world. However, we need to go back a little bit farther in time than that because we need to talk about the idea. The right idea, of course, is the most crucial part of starting a business. When I say *the right idea*, it does not mean what society will want or what the community will want. It has to be the one idea that is the most fun for the entrepreneur. It is the one that they are most passionate about. Most people and most books will say to take a hobby and turn it into a business, and that is fine. However, sometimes the hobbies people want to turn into businesses will not generate the revenue necessary to pay bills or provide a decent lifestyle. It could make for extra income if they wanted to do it part-time.

The idea is crucial. It sometimes has to be modified or transformed to fit a niche, but if there is a passion behind it and a big enough market, it should fly. Then it is time to test the idea. There are several ways of doing this. One test is to tell people about the business idea. Now, I know, I get it, people do not want other people to steal their ideas, so they feel compelled to give only half information or not to tell the full story, and I understand that need for security. If entrepreneurs are creating businesses in a highly competitive field, then that is true. Technology is one of those industries where brand new *things* being created need a higher level of security while inventors are obtaining patents. This will require working with lawyers and other trusted people. However, in most cases, there are no new ideas. If it does not already exist, there is a reason. It is too expensive, somebody has already tried it and failed, the community or industry does not want it, or it could be that nobody has even tried it. All the reasons have to be explored as to why it does not exist. If it does exist, there is more than likely current competition. Research needs to be conducted to see what the competition is already doing.

Sometimes people think that because they are good at something, then that is the type of business that will fly. For example, let's say their passion is cooking. Their first thought is to open a restaurant or start a catering company. Initially, I would advise them to research the community they want to do business in and find out how many restaurants and catering companies there are. A little research could show that the community needs a certain type of restaurant because there is only fast food in that town. Perhaps locals would like to have more sit-down dining, maybe there is no place to eat a good breakfast, or they would like to have a venue that has a bar, or they would welcome a kid-friendly eatery. There are many ways to conduct research, but the easiest is to just look in the community or in the area where the business is going to be located. If 30 different restaurants currently exist with varied cuisine, differences in size, quality, and social status, then a restaurant may not be the best business idea for that area and could be quite a costly failure. The only way this can truly be figured out is by doing a feasibility study.

They Like It. They Really Like It!

The feasibility study starts, like I said, with looking in the community and talking to people. Do the people like the idea? The most important thing about this process is listening to the answers. Being defensive or upset with what they say will get the project nowhere. Make sure to listen objectively. To be honest, relatives tend to be the most straightforward. Filter out the good information from the concerned information when enlisting the help of family members. A filter is necessary because sometimes mothers, fathers, wives, or husbands are saying what they are saying because they do not want you to get hurt. They do not want you to take a risk or at least they want you to be extremely careful. So sometimes you will hear "Do you really want to get into that?" or "Is this really the best idea for you?" I have seen that when husbands, wives, girlfriends, and boyfriends have discussed an idea, many times they are the most critical, not of the person, but of the idea. Listen to it. It tends to be some of the best feedback that you can hear. Other times, you just need to hear it from the public.

Aaron was a student at a local university. He believed that he had the best idea for a clothing store that would cater specifically to young college women. His idea was to have a custom T-shirt shop where these young women could come in, create a design, have it converted into a decal, and have it placed wherever they wanted it on a T-shirt of their choice. He was also going to contract with local artists to create one-of-a-kind designs that would then be transferred onto T-shirts and sell them at a higher price because they would be considered "art."

Aaron had a retail space all picked out close to the campus and had even spoken to the landlord about a rental agreement. He created his pricing structure to coincide with his unique merchandise. He believed that he would be able to sell the "create your own" T-shirt for $50 because customers would have made it themselves and would cherish their own work enough to pay the higher price. He was also going to sell the one-of-a-kind shirts for $75 each because they were considered pieces of art. He believed that the "one-of-a-kind" aspect was worth the increase in price.

When Aaron and I started discussing his idea, he was extremely excited about having found a niche market that he believed would provide a product to young college women, make him some money, and, he admitted later, find him a new girlfriend. After all he figured he would have several hundred women coming into his store every week to purchase his merchandise. Sure one of them would take an interest in him. Hey, some of the reasons for becoming an entrepreneur are not always about freedom and potential income.

Once we got back on track, I began to ask him about his retail background and what he knew about the clothing and textile industry. He admitted he had little to no education or experience in either retail or the clothing market. I asked about his pricing structure and if he knew for a fact the female college population would pay that amount for a T-shirt. He again had to admit that he did not know for sure if his pricing model was correct. I asked him to please conduct a feasibility study before he signed a rental agreement he potentially would not be able to afford.

Aaron agreed that he needed to do his research and find out everything he could about his business, industry, and target market before he spent the money to get it started. He checked out his competition, spoke to local artists to see how many would be interested in his venture, and stood in the student union with a clipboard asking female passersby their opinion on his idea. When he reported back to me, he was less than happy.

He had discovered there were 15 specialty clothing retail shops in the area where he wanted to do business and over 100 within the city limits. He learned that his prices were well beyond what customers would pay for the T-shirts by almost 60%. He could not get any local artist to commit to his project either. But the most telling feedback that he received was that not 1 out of the almost 150 respondents he talked to on campus would consider shopping at a T-shirt shop where they had to create the design or pay the price for the "artwork" shirts. They told him that it would be so much easier to go to the mall and shop for a designer shirt that would be priced within their budgets. His idea was a bust. When 0 out of 150 say no, that is a pretty solid response. Although a bit dejected, he was not completely down and out. What he realized was that the little bit of time it took to complete his feasibility study, two weeks total, saved him several thousand dollars he would have spent on a lease and merchandise plus saved him quite a few sleepless nights to boot.

Normally in a case like this, we would try to find a better way to launch the business based off the information received in the surveys and researched information. Many times the original idea may not have legs, but something new and viable pops up in the process. With the type of numbers he received in his survey, shifting the business to fit the need of the target wasn't even possible. In addition, Aaron realized that his lack of knowledge in the retail and clothing industries was also going to be a huge detriment. So he decided he would go back to what he loved, music and was still on the lookout for a new girlfriend.

Feasibility studies are a great and useful tool. Entrepreneurs can pay a lot of money to have a firm conduct a feasibility study for them. However, I do not like the idea of having another company do a study for someone else's business (especially when we are not talking about a multi-million dollar start-up), because it is not *their* business. The research company is going to compile a list of statistics regarding the industry, labor, economic development, and other business indicators. Sometimes the best way to know what all that means is to do it yourself. There are many websites that can provide helpful information. There are resources that are available. Information for a study can be obtained at the local small business development center and at some community colleges. Entrepreneurs can also go to the Small Business Administration, universities, and the public library to find out all of the information needed about the industry. The Chamber of Commerce is also an excellent resource. They can give information on local development and the types of businesses that are needed in that area.

Talk to people. Conduct surveys to see whether people would actually use the product or service. This tool can also help figure out if the pricing structure is right. So make sure to ask questions about pricing. These questions could be as simple as *How much would you pay for a bowl of soup if you had a soup-only restaurant? Would you pay $10 for it?* I doubt it, but you never know. It depends on the area and competitive pricing. If it is a darned good bowl of soup, then maybe they will pay *$10* for it. You just never know until you ask the questions.

The feasibility study can be formal or information. It is up to the entrepreneur. In most cases, the basic questions researched in a feasibility study are as follows:

- Is the product or service something that people want?
- Is it something that they will pay for?
- Will they seek out this product or service?
- Who are the people who will seek out and pay for this product?
- Where are they located?
- Who else does what I want to do?
- Where are they located?
- How much do they charge for the same or similar product or service?

(Just a side note, the target market is never everyone—I repeat, it is *never* everyone. That is marketing money thrown out of the window. That just does not make good business sense. In addition, the competition is also *never* nobody.) Knowledge is power. The feasibility study should reveal usable information about the product, service, target market, price, industry, and of course, competition.

There is always competition, even if the new business is not exactly like existing ones. Let's say the business idea is a mobile motorcycle repair company, with no shop. The repair vehicle comes to the client at their place of business, their house, or in a parking lot—wherever their motorcycle is, that is where it is fixed. If there are no other businesses in town that offer this specific service, that is fine, but that does not mean there is no competition. The competition will more than likely be with other people who fix motorcycles. Customers just have to go to where they are located, and they may do that because they know them and like their work. That is the competition—other people who fix motorcycles. Another form of "competition" that most everyone has, especially in an elastic business, is potential customers choosing to save rather than spend. People will do that, especially in bad economic times, so that is when marketing becomes especially important.

If a feasibility study concludes that there is really no market for the product that does not mean the idea is dead in the water. It is more difficult and costly, but a market can be created for that product or service by creating the want. If nobody has ever heard of, let's say, life coaching in a particular region of the country and the goal is to open a life coaching center, buzz can be created so people can figure out that they want a life coach. It takes more time, it takes more money, but it can be done. If there is a passion for the idea and the entrepreneur has the drive to get it done, then almost anything can happen. There has to be an understanding that it is going to be more work if there is not already a need or a want out there for what is being created. That is the great part of a feasibility study—it should show the path to success.

Regarding listening to feedback from the surveys, sometimes the idea that has been suggested does not seem appealing to the participants. Again, this does not mean the idea is impractical. Because the idea has been rolling around in the entrepreneur's brain for so long, and they think it is awesome, they may be the only person who thinks it is the best idea on this planet. But they have to make sure they are creating something that other people want. If the idea is not quite what the surveyed public wants it to be, then it should be adjusted to meet or exceed expectations, or changed up a little so it has a better appeal to the consumer. It has to be something that can be put out in the world that people are going to love. More importantly, they are going to spend money on it. Flexibility helps maintain the original principle behind the idea, but allows for alteration for consumer acceptance.

A completed feasibility study will provide demographic and target market data, industry knowledge, and identification of the competition. The entrepreneur will know more about the product and service, as well as the service area. All of this information is necessary for proper planning of the business.

Planning Can Be Fun

Planning how the business will operate is necessary before you open the doors. Once, I conducted a three-hour workshop on the basics of starting a business. I talked about the initial steps, evaluating the business idea, the feasibility study, the planning and funding, and understanding the target market and the industry. I also provided several other ideas and hints that people needed to know when starting a business. At the end of the three hours, a gentleman named Wilbur looked at me and said, "That is all very nice, but I don't want to do all that. I just want to start a business." He said, "All I want to do is move scrap metal. That's all. I know other people who have started businesses before and they just went out and did it."

I had to explain that the reason why he should do a feasibility study and business planning is that today we can no longer do it like we did 25 or 30 years ago. It cannot be done. We cannot afford to take the risk—the financial risk—that we were able to take back then because the risk is bigger and therefore we can lose our valuable assets more easily. We have to be solid in our ideas and in our planning so that the risk is minimal for the entrepreneurs and their families, or anybody who is dependent on them. We have to take the time, to go through the steps. It is no longer practical to say, "Hey, I'm in business. I want to go for it," and then go.

The Horrifying yet Real Adventures of Henry

A young gentleman, Henry, came to see me. He was maybe 21 years old, if that. He sat down across from me at my desk with a sullen look on his face. I asked him why he was coming to see me. He said, "I need to learn how to start and run a business." He went on to tell me he was an expert in auto detailing. I began a question-based interview after telling him that auto detailing was a wonderful skill and very marketable. We talked for a bit and then he dropped the full story. He said, quietly, "Well, the thing is, I've already had this business. I just need to know how to do it right." He went on to tell me he had taken one class in auto detailing, and he had someone tell him that he was pretty good at it and that he should start a business. So he did. After one class of auto detailing and no business experience mind you, he decided to start his own business. He found a location with the bays he needed to do the work, and with a little bit of money, he was able to secure it. He knew he needed help during the busy times so he hired his friends to work for him because they all needed jobs. Then he hired a CPA to do his books because he did not know anything about bookkeeping. I asked him why he was sitting in front of my desk at that point, and he said, "Because I went bankrupt..." There was a long pause. Then he finished, "I had to file for bankruptcy because my business went under."

He said, "I didn't know what I was doing. The first thing I did wrong was hire my friends. They did not respect me as a boss or an owner. They did what they wanted and whenever I asked them to do something different or come in to work on time. They just brushed off what I asked them to do and did their own thing. There was no respect there." He continued, "The second bad thing I did was ... I did not know how to price myself correctly. I was priced way too low, plus I did not know how to collect what was owed when people didn't pay. The last thing I did wrong was I hired a CPA. I'm not saying that a CPA is wrong, but sometimes you can overdo something. I needed a bookkeeper." He needed an accountant—somebody who could take care of his books and pay taxes for him. CPAs cost a lot of money. He said that the one thing that was kind of a slap in the face was that they charged him a $150 to write him the letter to tell him that he had to file for bankruptcy.

He admitted to me that he did not run his business right. This time around he was going to make sure he knew what he was doing. He was going to take classes, ask for help, and follow business start-up procedures. He learned from his mistakes. After further discussions, he decided the best plan of action was to do an apprenticeship with a business owner so he would understand what it meant to be in business. At some point, he will successfully start his own business. That is a perfect example why business planning and conducting feasibility studies are necessary. We just cannot take those kinds of risks anymore. At 21 years old, he filed bankruptcy, and lost everything.

Suck It Up and Do It

If I am working with a client who is starting a completely new business, I want to know they are looking beyond the first year. Generally, most first-time entrepreneurs get stuck in the start-up phase. They cannot visualize anything past opening day or the first few months. I want to know that they are envisioning things up to and beyond three years. That helps me understand their mindset. I want them to be thinking, "Okay, once I get this done, what's the next step?" They should be working on their business today, but thinking about what they can be doing for it tomorrow. If they cannot tell me anything about the future, then that is an area that needs work.

I often get the business owners who are focused on opening their doors, and then they jump to the day they no longer have to work there every day. They want to have 10 employees in two locations and to be making enough money to go off on vacation whenever they want. They are missing a very important part—all of the work in the middle that is going to get them out of the business and on vacation. We talk numbers. I ask them to figure out how much income they need to be able to pay someone to run everything for the business. Then I ask them how long it will take at their current rate of growth to get them to that dollar amount. This is where they start to see reality.

Once reality has set in, marketing strategies are next on the agenda. I want to know what they are planning to do or are currently doing to get the word out about their business. New business owners do not always understand that even though they are not currently in business, they have to start marketing prior to opening the doors. It can be as simple as telling everyone, "I'm in business." They have to start that marketing process early. In this day and age, it is crucial that marketing is completed, that it is handled diligently, and that they commit to it. I want them to create a demand for their product or service prior to being in business; make it feel in-elastic or a need. This will help ensure a revenue stream from day one. Most of this publicity is done through traditional marketing, with networking as one of the best approaches.

I know that business planning is a task that tends to send shivers down people's spines, but business plans have to be written. It does not have to be done through formal classes, seminars, or workshops; it just has to be done. I tell entrepreneurs they have to do this, especially if they have never been in business before. If they do not know how any of the processes work, then by all means, sit down and take the time to write a formal business plan. If entrepreneurs do know how the business process works, they can create a less formal plan. No matter what, a plan must be created.

If any kind of funding is needed, then a business plan has to be written. No funder out there today will just say, "Okay, here you go. Here's fifteen thousand dollars, go open your business." They want to see a written business plan with accurate financial projections. They want to know due diligence has been done. The tone of the plan has to be as if it is going to happen tomorrow. There is no wishing or hoping in it either. It will either happen or it will not. Almost every funder I know reads the executive summary of a business plan, and then turns to the financial pages because the financial pages will tell them the story of the business just as much as all the written stuff that is in the middle. Most operations specialists, marketers, and coaches read the plan from beginning to end.

Many times if there is no need for funding or if the details just need to be expressed, all that really has to be written is a detailed executive summary and the financials. That should help get the business plan out of the entrepreneur's head and onto paper. In this detailed summary, it is necessary to show an understanding of all the components of starting a business, including:

- The company background and location
- The products and services
- The pricing, industry, and competition (all of which should have been learned from the feasibility study)
- Knowledge of the market and industry
- The specific target market(s)
- How the projected consumer receives their information. Every demographic is different. Twenty-something's get their information very differently than those in their thirties or fifties or seventies.
- Marketing and selling strategies. Selling can be done in many different ways. It will depend on what is being sold, who it is being sold to, and if it is a retail location, online, or direct sales.
- How the business will operate and who will manage it.
- The financial makeup of the company

While working on their plan, I always ask clients to find a location where they would like to have their business and learn how much it would cost to rent or buy that space. Whether they eventually locate there or not does not matter. What matters is that they have gone to a physical location to learn what the area looks like, when the other businesses in the neighborhood are open, how the traffic pattern works, and maybe even what the utility costs might be. At the very least they have put a physical "face" to their place of business. And if they were diligent, they probably talked to a real estate agent, a landlord, or somebody who can help them purchase a building or rent a spot, and learned about that process. After doing all of this, they may not know everything they need to know but will at least have a good idea what it should cost to keep the doors open. This information will also help them when it comes to pricing their product or service. The hard costs of doing business must always be built into the price.

Without proper planning, most people tend to believe they will go straight from idea generation and start-up to counting the profits. Most forget that day-to-day operation needs to occur to create revenue. These operational basics also have to be identified during the planning process. How the business operates cannot be lodged in the entrepreneur's head. It has to be on paper, especially if there is a partner or an employee involved. The operations section of the business plan outlines the day-to-day operations. Entrepreneurs are not writing an operating manual, but just showing they have an understanding of what to expect. If the business is retail, write down what hours the business will be open. Will it be 7 days a week, 24 hours a day? Is it only going to be open from seven to four with Monday's off? The point is the hours of operation have to be known.

Operations—Not Just a Fun Board Game

Another component of the business to think about is how many employees there are going to be. Will there be specific employee divisions or will they all be under one umbrella? Most entrepreneurs cannot even believe they would ever have an employee, let alone several. I tell them that sure, right now they may not want or need one, but what happens when the business grows? What happens when they would like to take a vacation? They must think about this because the business generally grows at a faster pace than they anticipate and employees become a reality sooner rather than later. It just means that at some point they have to know what it will mean to be an employer. If so:

- What kind of work history, education, and character traits would you want in an employee?
- Would you plan to carefully supervise an employee or do you need someone who can work independently?

- Will you need a full-time or a part-time employee? What are the advantages and disadvantages of each?
- What benefits can you offer? (Remember that nonmonetary benefits like a flexible schedule or training can be valuable, depending on the employee's situation.)
- Where is the cash register going to be and who will have control of the cash?
- Do you need retail space, or just an office building?
- Will you create an interactive work space? Or will there cubicles? Individual office spaces?
- Is there sufficient lighting, bathrooms, and quiet space? Who handles the trash collection, pays the utilities, and cleans?
- Will there be too much residual noise when all of the employees are in the space at the same time?
- Where will you hold meetings? Where will you and employees meet with clients?

When most people look at potential business space, they only think, "My desk can go here and my computer can go on top of that, and I will have a filing cabinet here," but:

- What about storage?
- Where will the inventory go? Is there inventory? Is it "just-in-time inventory," the current inventory practice of choice?
- Is there enough room for expansion? How much can your business grow and still be able to function in this space?

There are so many things that have to be thought about with operations. Every business is different, so you have to know what it would look like.

Know Your Numbers—Know Yourself

Understanding the financials is crucial. Entrepreneurs have to be able to create an income statement, a balance sheet, and a cash flow statement. If they do not know or like accounting, then they had better figure out who can help them with it. There are many business financial templates out there. SCORE.org has free templates for business plans and for the cash flow statements, income statements, and balance sheets. Remember, in addition to doing the financial reports, you will probably need an accountant for help with your taxes. If an accountant is not available, then find someone with a finance background who understands how to put financial reports together.

On the other hand, knowledge is power. There are many workshops out there on the basics of accounting, and on QuickBooks and other accounting products that will help track the business financially. Knowing how all of the numbers get into the spreadsheets helps to understand the financial reports generated from those spreadsheets. In the first year, it is essential to know what every month's numbers look like, from rent to marketing to operational expenses and labor. If there are employees, worker's compensation is a required payment, as is unemployment insurance. Entrepreneurs will also need to get statistical information about the taxes for their area.

Creating Opportunities and Making Connections over Cocktails

In addition to knowing about the business, the business idea, the things that are going on, maybe some of the day-to-day functions, and a little bit about the challenges and the successes, entrepreneurs must begin interacting with their competition. Being acquaintances with or in networking groups with the competition can help in so many ways. Many times competitors become allies. They can refer customers, help with marketing strategies, and can even create an alliance to bring new products to the region. These new competitive relationships will also provide a connection with people who could become their clients.

In today's entrepreneurial world, networking ranks high on the list of things to do to succeed. Many local networking organizations can help new and existing business owners create interest in their businesses. There are also small business associations, local chambers, professional networking groups, and industry organizations.

Small business associations and local chambers serve a similar purpose. They bring together business owners normally located in the same general vicinity. These groups will provide social activities, training sessions, economic development information, and introduce new opportunities for members. They tend to be the main information resource for all of their members and create ways for all of the business owners to interact to create working relationships.

Networking groups help business owners showcase their businesses and products. They help them create specific business strategies based off of information gained and partnerships created. They are also designed to generate leads for the members as well as be a pipeline for legal issues that can affect small business owners. However, the biggest benefit to joining networking groups is the camaraderie. Think about it. Networking groups are chock-full of people cut from the same cloth. Networking groups not only bring together business owners for business reasons but also take all of those entrepreneurs off their isolating islands and create a community of like-minded individuals.

Industry groups allow business owners to mingle with their competition. They also showcase new products and tend to attract subsidiary organizations as well.

It's important that entrepreneurs know who they are working with and competing against!! Joining an industry group is also one of the best ways to know the heavy hitters in the industry and who can become an ally to gain clients.

In addition to knowing about products and services, marketing and targets, and every other component of the business plan, entrepreneurs need to know how the business is going to end. I know this is tough to think about when the business is not even started yet, but it must be done. There are several options for ending a business. Will it be sold soon after it starts to turn a profit? Is it your baby and you plan to run it for the next 30 years, and then close it so nobody else can have it? Or is the plan to run it for 20 or 30 years, then sell it, or maybe will it to somebody? Maybe somebody in the family would like to come in and take the business over. It is completely up to the entrepreneur, but he or she has to know how this business will end. In this day and age, one thing that community leaders frown on is entrepreneurs just closing the doors to their businesses. They want to make sure that if there is a successful business in the community that people have been enjoying for many years, it stays there.

It takes longer to sell a business than most people think, which means that if they want to retire next year, it is probably not going to happen. They had better start the valuation process about five years prior to when they want to retire. This is called succession planning. This plan specifies how the business is going to be turned over to somebody else or sold. The plan might mean bringing in the new owner six months to a year to understand the ins and outs of the business before the owner decides to leave. It is not a split-second decision and is not like selling a car, or even selling a house. Selling and valuing a business is extremely difficult and a business owner has to know well in advance when that will happen.

When entrepreneurs are getting ready to start a business, there are things that they can do. They can take classes and workshops, or seek a formal education through an accredited school, college, or university. However, before they take any classes or workshops, their idea must be solid. They should know it well enough to explain it to other people. Entrepreneurs have to talk about their idea and tell people what they want to do. Then they have to write a plan of some sort about their business and how to make it operational. Then they build it, create it, launch it, and make it go. The only way to make a business successful is for people to actually *do* the business. There are so many people out there who will help and there are so many resources available, but none of them can launch a business. It takes courage, and hard work, but it can be done. I know it can. I see it happen all the time.

Chapter 10

What Is Your Time Worth?

Pricing is tough no matter what kind of business you are in. There are generally two types of businesses, those that sell a product or a series of products and those that sell a service. The businesses that sell products have a leg up when it comes to pricing because they know the cost of goods sold. The retail price is made up of the cost of the inventory, adding on the hard costs of doing business such as rent and utilities and finally a percentage for profit. A quick comparison with competitor's prices and the product can go on the market.

Service-based businesses are a different story. At start-up, most service-based businesses are underpriced. The thought process is that if the service is sold at a lower price, more people will buy it. When working with service-based entrepreneurs, I ask them:

- What are you worth?
- What is your time worth?
- What do you believe is ample compensation for experience, talent, and time?
- What price tag do you want to hang on your abilities?

They generally do not have an answer for that right away because most have never really thought of themselves as having the type of talent people would pay a lot of money for. They just know that they know how to clean floors, mow lawns, or paint houses. They think that by marketing a price lower than their competitors, they will gain more clients. What they often find out is that they are selling themselves short and are not making enough money to run their businesses.

Eventually, many over time figure out that customers will judge a business by their prices. If entrepreneurs come in well below the competition, the customer will often think that something is wrong with the business or that service is substandard. That is not a reputation that business owners want.

I always emphasize that their talents, time away from their families, their education, and their experiences are all worth something and all of that needs to be built into their prices. I also have them research the pricing structure of their competition. This gives them a good starting point for their own prices. One young gentleman I worked with, Danny, had a curb painting business. He had the hardest time trying to figure out how to price his service. He thought that if his prices were too high, people would not hire him to paint their curbs. He knew what other people were charging in town and felt he could offer a much better price for his customers. To come up with the best pricing strategy, he calculated the cost of goods sold. He started by taking inventory of all the supplies for a typical curb painting job: one can of paint, reflective glass crystals, stencils, and decals. The hardest part was getting him to understand that he also had to price his talent and time.

Obtaining information about the paint was easy because the paint company stated how many square feet each spray can would paint. That made the price breakdown by curb much easier. He mapped out all of the processes for the business, starting with the creation of marketing, to sales, and finally the painting of the curbs. I wanted Danny to understand that he had to take every moment in his business into consideration when creating a price structure. The most difficult concept for him to accept was that his time was worth something even when he went door to door trying to sell his service. In addition, he needed to understand that the time he was taking to paint was also worth something in dollars. He finally figured out that his time *was* worth something when he underbid a parking lot job. He underbid it so badly that he did not have enough money to pay for all of the paint that he needed for the handicapped signs and parking lines. In fact, in that case, he had to go back to the property owner to see whether he could re-bid the project. This part was scary for him because he knew he could lose the contract. Fortunately they liked him and allowed him to submit another proposal, which they accepted. In hindsight he agreed that even his second quote was still too low, but he got the job done and after that was more diligent in the bidding and pricing process.

Can You Put a Price on Talent?

Figuring out time in dollars and cents tends to be a daunting task. Entrepreneurs tend to undervalue themselves. Along with that goes the difficulty in pricing their creativity and talents, especially artistic abilities.

A young artist, Jacob, came to me to figure out how much his drawings were worth. Jacob had been drawing for fun for many years. He is quiet and shy, but knows that his ability to draw could make him money. He started his career by drawing tattoos for his friends, but wanted to break the reputation of being only a tattoo artist. His pencil and ink drawings tended to be on the dark side, lots of skulls and bones, and were attractive to a specific demographic that usually did not have the kind of income necessary to pay for the quality of work Jacob produced. His goal was to create one-of-a-kind pieces that could be showcased on clothing. He knew there was a demand for this type of product if he could get noticed by the right market.

I asked him how long it took to make one drawing. He thought a moment and told me each piece took approximately 20 hours to complete. Then we started breaking down the process of creating his work into pencils, pens, ink, paper, and other supplies. I then wanted to know how many art classes he had taken. These courses would be considered an investment in his talent. Once he had all of that information in front of him, he started evaluating his current pricing structure. He was not putting a price on any of his talent at all, only the cost of his supplies.

To help him understand that pricing talent and time was important, I had him meet with a couple of different artists who did commissioned paintings for a living. I wanted him to talk to them to see how they did their pricing because they definitely charged for what they could do. Both the artists agreed that most people could not do what they do. They create beautiful things that can last a lifetime. That type of talent needs to be priced accordingly. They both told Jacob their starting prices and why they thought what they charged was fair. Having Jacob meet these two artist entrepreneurs provided him with an understanding that his time, his efforts, and his talents really were worth something. He then created a pricing structure for his work based off of the information he gained. In my opinion, it was still too low, but he is comfortable quoting the prices to clients.

If entrepreneurs undervalue themselves, they give away their talent. I understand when they are starting out that sometimes they have to provide *samples* of their service and monetary perks to be noticed, such as a free bill-pay for all new accounting clients. However, the preference is to never give away service unless it is for charity. I am a firm believer that entrepreneurs should never give away the farm before it is built. Service for trade or in-kind, on the other hand, is a completely different story. If they happen to need a computer, sometimes free accounting for a year is an adequate trade to pay for that new computer.

I worked with a local hydroponic lettuce grower to finalize his business plan to go after funding for the new greenhouse he needed to expand his business. When I asked how much he was currently harvesting, he said he was getting about 40 heads of lettuce a week. When I asked the price per head and said it was $1 a head. So his revenue was $40 a week. He agreed it would be $40 a week if he was actually charging people for the lettuce he was distributing. I was shocked by that answer.

I went on to ask why he was not charging for the 40 heads of lettuce he was delivering. His answer was twofold. He said he wanted to "get his lettuce out there" so that when he did start charging people would know the quality and would really want it. The second part of his answer was that the people receiving his lettuce were friends and family and he just did not feel right charging them. I told him that if he ever wanted to show potential funders he had a viable business, he needed to show a revenue stream. From that day forward, he *sold* his lettuce. Not one of his family members or friends dropped off as a customer just because they had to pay a dollar for the lettuce.

I understand that creating pricing structures can sometimes be difficult. Most new entrepreneurs firmly believe that a low price will get them clients. When it comes to pricing, my rule of thumb is that if entrepreneurs are getting all *yes's* when they quote their prices, then the price is too low. When they start getting *no's* that means they are getting closer to the right price strategy. If about 30% to 35% of potential customers say no, the prices are pretty much on point. Of course, they have to make sure their pricing is competitive. They also want people to get a good value for that price. It is possible to price effectively and get paid for a job well done.

Chapter 11

Cameras Are Not the Only Things that Should Be Focused

All entrepreneurs need to write one word on the wall directly in their view while they are working. It is not passion, spirit, drive, or success. The word is Focus! All entrepreneurs, whether they are just starting out or have been in business for years, need to have focus. When entrepreneurs get busy working to gain clients, they sometimes lose focus by promising outcomes that are outside their scope of service, or sometimes they are just too busy chasing that almighty dollar to understand that they are taking their business in a direction that could eventually be detrimental to its success. They want to please their customers and make sure they come back. They believe they can do anything the customer requests. Once they start saying yes to services outside their business structure, the lines blur and the picture gets fuzzy. They wake up one morning wondering what their business is really about and what it really offers.

When a company is just starting out, laying out the exact product line or service offering is crucial. Those products and services will be the center of all the marketing, sales, and eventually, accounts receivable. New business owners sometimes think that just because they have the ability or talent to do something they should go ahead and do it for a client, whether it is on their list of services or not. However, just because the know-how is there does not mean they should be performing that service for the client.

When working with a startup tech company, I first asked the two partners what services they provided in their business. The answer was, "Anything having to do with technology. We can fix computers, write programs, create websites, help businesses with their IT solutions, troubleshoot IT problems, run cabling, and supply business or individuals with new hardware." I agreed that that was quite impressive, but wanted to know what their business services were, not what they could do. I received a blank stare that said, "We just told you!" I explained that just because they had the ability to perform all of those tasks did not mean their company had to provide all of them. Before they left the meeting, I asked them to look at all of their immediate competition to see what services they provided. I asked them to specifically note the length of the lists.

After several months of marketing their business, networking, and taking on new clients, the pair returned looking exhausted. I asked how everything was going and received a positive yet somewhat exasperated response that things were great, but not what they expected. They found that by offering such a wide variety of services, they were so busy that they were not having any fun doing work that they usually enjoyed. I asked if they had done their homework regarding their competition. They said each of the companies they aspired to be like had two or three main products or services with one or two secondary services. I wanted to know what those companies did with a work request they could not fill. They apparently referred the client to a company they knew performed that service well. I asked if they were a referral company for any of their competitors, and they said, "No, because we do not specialize."

At that point, they agreed they needed to create a focus for their business that was not currently being met by their competitors. I had them create a list of the services they liked to perform and the ones they would prefer that someone else did. They both agreed they liked web design and solving IT problems. They also knew that they wanted to help small businesses either in the launch stage or early growth. Focusing the business services on the areas of specific interest to the pair made them much happier. They were also serving clients who were very similar to themselves, so they understood what was going on in the businesses and could make recommendations that were beneficial. They also knew they had skills in other areas that could come in handy if they ever wanted to extend a one-time offer to a client they particularly liked.

After streamlining the services for the business, the tech company became easier to market, sparking more growth. They were able to refer clients to their competitors, gaining respect as a solid tech company with a niche market and specialty services. Showing their competitors they were a solid company, they became a referral option for them as well.

In some cases, focus becomes extremely difficult for business owners and trying to steer them back to the correct path is virtually impossible. For some entrepreneurs, the focus of the business services is not the issue. The real issue is within themselves. Some entrepreneurs are "idea generators." They come up with idea after idea of businesses they want to pursue and will stray from a business venture that they are in the process of starting or growing. This idea generating talent may not be so bad if the ideas generated fall in line with their current business and could potentially provide future growth. However, in some cases, the ideas they feel they have to pursue are in a completely different market than their current business. When this failure to focus occurs, it tends to be detrimental to both the business that is growing and the new business they want to start.

In one such instance, a human resources expert decided to leave her corporate position to help small companies who needed a human resources consultant but did not need or want to hire one permanently. The idea was well received by the small business community and very quickly the self-appointed queen of human resources was born. The business struggled only slightly in the beginning, but was well on its way to being a success in a very short time. She provided hiring training and helped create job descriptions and employee manuals. She would even sit in on an interview panel after writing all of the interview questions. Her pricing was fair, but she was adequately paid for her talent and time. Many people believed this business would be a success and were waiting for her to grow and starting hiring new employees herself.

The shocker came one day when out of the blue she told me she no longer wanted to be in the human resources industry. She wanted to become a caterer instead. She felt her ability to work with people was being wasted on trivial problems that seemed depressing. She believed her talents would be better used creating parties for corporations and providing succulent pastries and desserts. When asked if she had experience, education, or background in catering, her response was "no," but she knew she could do it because she had worked for a caterer in college. She also knew there was a need for corporate catering because many of her clients brought it up when working with her on their human resources issues. She believed she would be able to go to all of those same clients and have them hire her to do all their catering just as they had done with their human resources needs. She hadn't just shifted gears—she had driven down a completely different road.

This entrepreneur did not change logo or company slogan. Nor did she change the website or contact information. All that was changed was the company name. She believed that having everything look the same would show her clients that she was still the same respectable business owner, just with a new service to offer. What she failed to consider in this radical shift was that her previous clients hired her for her abilities as a human resources expert. Her insight in human resources was spot on, and she had an incredible ability to talk with people and make them feel warm and welcome. These former clients knew nothing of her abilities to cater and so most did not hire her for their functions. She also did not consider that creating human resources consulting business was essentially an inexpensive startup because there were no real assets to purchase. Her biggest asset was her knowledge and her experience. Catering requires a large capital outlay for all of the equipment necessary to serve food to a large group of people. Unfortunately, this lack of focus led to the demise of two businesses. However, do not feel bad for her. As a person who generates ideas often, she has already moved on to her next venture, creating funding channels for nonprofit organizations, and is doing quite well.

Focus is essential for business owners. Sometimes they have to be yanked by the collar and forced to take a step back to see where their business is going and what effect the wrong decision can have on their success. They often learn how to focus when they become tired and see that they are not making any money.

Chapter 12

What If This Actually Works? Handling Growth

I absolutely love it when entrepreneurs talk about ways to grow their businesses. They are so energized and bubbling over with excitement about their new ideas. Seeing the passion in their eyes and hearing them talk about where their business could go, figuring out new and different paths they could follow and the problems they have to conquer—it's fun to be working with them. Knowing all of that, my job as a coach is to make sure that this new addition to their venture is realistic or will it mess up what they have already accomplished. I need to ensure that everything they want to do makes sense for the business, so I ask:

- Is this the next logical step?
- Does it stay within your mission?
- What are the possible financial gains?
- How will it affect your work–life balance?
- Do you have the funding for it?

Any time entrepreneurs come to me with ideas that are new and exciting, but sound like they just do not fit with their current mission, I have to delve into those ideas. I want to know the inspiration for this new vein and why they think it is worth pursuing. I want to make sure it is really worth trying because if it goes bad, it could be detrimental to the business, and the last thing they need is an ill-timed financial burden. If it does go bad, the result could alienate customers or give a bad reputation to the company and the entrepreneur. They have to be very careful when evaluating these new ideas. Most of the time and with a few modifications, the idea is feasible. When they approach me with this grand new idea, I say, "Okay, let's step back and look at it from all sides. Let's try to figure out the best direction for it to go." Having them take this moment to look at it from the viewpoint of the customer, the competition, or even the employees is beneficial because it makes them slow down before making any decisions. It makes them look at their inspirational idea as a business owner and think of the possibilities for a continued revenue stream. This is where the entrepreneurial growth happens. It will soon become instinct for them to take a quick yet thorough analysis of any new idea to see whether it has merit. If it looks good, then they should pursue it, if not ditch it.

Once the business owner has gone through the process of evaluating the new idea and has decided it will be a good addition to the product line or service menu, we discuss the long-term effects the addition will have on the business. Generally adding a new product will increase revenue and sales during the initial offering, but growth will plateau once the newness has worn off. However, this new addition could possibly be the one big boost that the company needs to take it to the next level. So I ask, "If you get a hundred new clients tomorrow, how is that going to affect your business? How are you going to handle it?"

The very first thing I see is the wheels turning in their heads because a hundred new clients means more money. Most entrepreneurs will take the thought process through the money route first, calculating how much revenue the new venture is going to bring in. But then the reality sinks in. The thought process then goes through the time and effort required by those hundred new clients and the manpower that will be needed. The reality sets in that they are a one-person operation with no additional assistance at hand. Then the fear comes across their faces because they realize that 100 brand new clients in one day could actually mean the loss of their business. Most new startups cannot handle that kind of rapid growth.

Many entrepreneurs cannot hire employees right away because they do not have the funding available. They have to do most of the work themselves, so having that much growth in that short of a time period will actually hurt them more than help them. There are not enough hours in the day to complete the orders. They cannot physically get all the work done in a suitable amount of time. As the old saying goes, "Be careful what you wish for..."

Business owners have to prepare for growth as best they can. They must try to grow the business at a measured rate so that they can add on resources as needed. This could mean hiring employees, conducting training sessions on the new product, acquiring funding, renting or buying additional facility space, and finding time to create all of the necessary processes. The upside to all of this is that once entrepreneurs have all of this in place, growth should not be an issue for them at all. They then can grow bigger faster and potentially land higher dollar clients. They can hire employees at a faster rate because all the processes are there. That fear leads to knowledge, which should make them a strong, confident entrepreneur.

A client, Ken, had the opportunity to work through this exact dilemma. He owns an online retail store catering to the niche market of golfers. He sells equipment such as balls, carrying cases and other supplies, and apparel. Ken knows his market very well as he is an avid golfer himself. He knew he could be successful because the type of store he created online was something he knew his fellow golfers needed. Even though he prepared for months conducting researching, creating his website, and lining up inventory distributers, he had no idea how much traffic to expect when he went live. We discussed the fact that a niche market site can go either way. It could be highly successful because it is needed in that market or it could draw minimal traffic because it is too specific. We also discussed the back-end processes that he would need to have in place such as database creation, order fulfillment, and responding to customer inquiries, but because he did not have any customers yet he could not visualize the complexity of the operation.

To Ken's delight, he had traffic on his site shortly after going live. He hoped this would happen because he had planned and rolled out marketing prior to the site being available. He placed ads on his distributor's websites and talked up his merchandise to his fellow golfers. Within the first three months of operations, his sales were triple his expectations. Ken continued with his marketing efforts to increase traffic to make sure the revenue he was experiencing was sustainable. He sponsored golf tournaments and posted sales on his site for merchandise. He even placed an ad in a golf magazine. Again, to his delight, the orders continued and even picked up in volume. This is when he discovered he had an issue. He could not fill the orders as quickly as they were coming in. He was constantly ordering inventory, answering e-mails, doing the daily bookwork, and then packaging orders long into the night. In addition, he was doing all of this from the spare room in the basement of his home.

His life was being consumed by the business he had created and his processes were beginning to break down. Ken couldn't meet his self-imposed deadlines for orders, he forgot/skipped/couldn't find time for meetings, and he did not update his website as regularly as his customers had come to expect. His wife tried to help when she could, but she had her own commitments to keep. He needed an employee. Ken put an ad in the local college paper for a part-time office assistant. When we talked, I asked what this person was going to be doing. His simple answer was, "Help run the business." I then asked what this person's duties were going to be. He said shrugged and just looked at me. I went on to ask how much he was going to pay this person. Again, he had no idea and for the most part had no idea if he had enough money to sustain this employee after he got past this ordering surge. Since the employment ad was already running in the paper, we sat down and tried to work out all of the details for the new hire.

After a lengthy discussion including salary, taxes, job descriptions, duties, and workspace needed, Ken figured out that he did not need someone who could fill orders. What he desperately needed was someone who could make the inventory changes and other updates to the website. He did not need an assistant at all. He needed a web designer or a web assistant. What he advertised for and what he needed were two very different things. The rush to hire almost cost him money that he was already having a hard time making. He cancelled the interviews and pulled the ad from the paper. Once he had the job description completed, Ken starting looking for an intern at the local community college. He created a small project that the interviewees could complete during the interview so that he could test their abilities and see whether they could work well together. Once he saw how they worked and to what level, he figured he could hire them if they have everything he needed. This process has worked well for him. He liked training the new intern and is happy to get a fresh perspective by bringing someone new into his business.

Chapter 13

Why Does Hiring Feel Like Dating?

Most entrepreneurs believe they need to have an employee the day they acquire 10 accounts, are a little frazzled, and feel they cannot get the work done. In their minds, they keep saying, "I need some help. I need some help. I need some help." Unbeknownst to them, that is not when they need the help. They have to learn how to cope with those pockets of chaos. They need to learn to manage their accounts, their time, and their processes. By the time they really do need help, they will understand that what they had just gone through was not nearly as stressful as when they actually become an employer.

Entrepreneurs do what they do because they like working on their own, being accountable for their own actions. Although being in their own offices may seem stressful at times, they understand everything that goes on in that world and they like it that way. When the time comes to hire an employee, they have to train him or her to do what they do. Becoming an employer requires a new skill set for the entrepreneur. It means being flexible, patient, and understanding. It means turning over a portion of the business to this new person. It also means measuring the outcomes based on the processes set forth. It *means* becoming a manager.

One common misconception when business owners hire employees is that they believe they have to set employee rules and duties based off what is expected in most corporations in their industries. For example, if they are in the web design industry, their first hire may be a programmer. The entrepreneur believes this is a basic hire for the company and creates a position for a programmer. They then scout for the best programmer in the industry or coming out of college. What the business owner fails to include in the job description are the other duties that go with the position. If they advertise for a programmer, that is what they will get: someone who expects to create code all day long. I am sure it would be a good hire, in the sense that this person knows how to program, and knows all of the most current programming languages. That is what a programmer does. However, most small business owners need more than a programmer. They need someone who can talk to the clients, up-sell products, and get a long-lasting customer by doing that extra little something the client was not expecting. They need someone who can answer the phone when the owner is not there, pick up the mail, monitor inventory, and most importantly, someone who has an entrepreneurial perspective.

Entrepreneurs must express what they truly need. If they advertise for graphic designer to fill a position, they are going to get a graphic designer. More often than not, what the new hire will want to do is design graphics all day long and that's about it. I encourage the entrepreneurs to come up with new names for the positions they are hiring for. I like "design associate" or "programmer extraordinaire." They can create a position title that best fits the job description. An oddly titled position will actually draw more attention because "account activist" looks very different than "account manager." The name alone shows creativity. Figuring out exactly what is needed in the business and then writing the job description to match that need is the way to go. The title can be eye-catching, but more importantly there has to be an employee in the end who will do everything that the entrepreneur needs him or her to do. Effective employees are a must in today's business world.

Jen, a previous client, and I were having coffee to get caught up on how things were going in her business. She informed me that she was ready to hire her "first real employee." She had had several interns and part-time employees come and go and was ready to hire someone who fit her needs and could be with her for the long haul. She needed someone who understood her business and work well with her. She expressed that she was nervous. She wanted it to be right this time.

I told her that hiring a good employee was a lot like dating. She had dabbled around with a few part-time "boyfriends," but now it was time to get serious and find someone who she wanted to be in a relationship with. She had her job description almost completed but did not know how to finish it. I told her that having an incomplete list was just fine. She knew what she needed that person to do, but what was great about this situation was not knowing what this new person was going to bring to the relationship. It was just like looking for a boyfriend. She knew mostly what she wanted in this relationship, but was hoping this person could bring attributes and experiences that she had never thought about. They may have work experience she never thought could be beneficial to her business.

As in dating, I told her she would never really know what she was getting until she met and talked to the person. Also as in dating, this "first real employee" should come with references or referrals. She needed to talk to colleagues to see whether they could "find her a good match" or "get her a phone number or two." She needed their help finding someone who could potentially be a good fit for her and her company. Once she has found someone she would like to meet, she should set up the interview. "It is similar to being set up on a blind date," I said. "You are not really sure what to expect. You only know what your friends have told you about this person. You hope he is Mr. Wonderful, but won't know for sure until you meet him." There has to be chemistry, a spark. If this occurs, then a second date is in order. If the chemistry is still there, then make an offer. Jen was amused by the metaphor and set off to find her Mr./Ms. Wonderful.

A match like this can benefit both parties. Entrepreneurs hire an individual who is willing to grow with the company. They add a component that they were possibly missing. The employees win because they have landed a position that allows them to express themselves. They can let their own entrepreneurial spirit shine while creating a career path for themselves and helping the businesses they work for grow.

Hiring Is Like Dating, Then Firing Must Be the Breakup!

Hiring ill-suited employees means having to let them go. "How do I fire an employee?" There is no easy way to do it. The usual human resource protocol is that everything leading up to the employee exit requires documentation. Employers can create their own gauges for measuring employees' infractions such as three strikes and they are out. Always remember to follow whatever your state laws require. Always make sure there is no discrimination in any way, shape, or form. Be certain that the employee really, truly has not completed the tasks at hand or worked at the standards set in their review or in the job description. Then all that is left to be done is letting them know and letting them go. Severance or no severance—there are many different ways to handle the departure. The details are up to the entrepreneur as long as it is legal, on the up and up, and documented.

Chapter 14

Aren't Good Intentions Enough?

Social entrepreneurship is on the rise. Many young people are talking about what they can do to give back to the community. Although noble, social ventures are not moneymakers by nature. They are designed to fulfill a need within an interest group or a community. Many social operations rely on volunteers. The majority of the funding generated by these organizations is dedicated to serving the community while fulfilling the mission. There are quite a few people who believe that social entrepreneurship is the way to go, and I commend them for this thought. Many want to be another "Tom's Shoes" and unfortunately that is not always realistic, especially if they are starting out with absolutely zero dollars in capital. They have to figure out a way to generate funding to help run the operations while they are in turn trying to promote this social mission.

As a coach, I will work with social entrepreneurs in the same manner as any other type of for-profit business owner. I ask about the inspiration for the idea and the intended outcome. Most answers are similar. They want to do it for the good of the community. When I ask about funding, most do not have any money or access to a funder. I explain to my client that starting a 501(c)3 is not an easy venture and requires a lot of time for very little pay, but with a huge reward. Most want to do it for the reward, not the income. Now, I know that there are nonprofits in the world that bring in a lot of money and have executives whose salaries are better than average. Those organizations are huge and help a wide range of causes that span the globe. Those types are different than somebody local who wants to save abused dogs or create a service for those individuals who cannot leave their homes but need help.

As I work with the potential owners, we discuss structure and funding. I point out that the majority of the money in the beginning will have to come from donors. I also call to their attention that nonprofits with no money and no reputation find it very difficult to get people to give to that organization because they want to know if it's reputable. There are too many scams these days that give honest nonprofit businesses a bad name. In addition, the competition is not for cause itself, but for dollars raised. The competition is not for the dogs and cats that are saved or for the women and children rescued from abusive environments, it is for the donations. Social ventures in today's world have to be run like any other businesses. Therefore, the person who is steering the ship needs to have a pretty decent business background and a grasp of everything that is going on in the community for fund-raising efforts. With hard work and dedication to the mission, all of these obstacles can be overcome. Nonprofits can flourish just like any other business, all while fulfilling a mission that will benefit the community.

Chapter 15

Entrepreneurship—Pass It On

Over the past 50 years, we have failed to teach our youth that entrepreneurship is an option. At the age of five, we start taking the risk out of their lives by doing everything for them and by giving them multiple choice tests in school. We also stifle the entrepreneurial spirit by removing all creativity from their lives and by overscheduling them. It is necessary in this day and age for children to fail. The problem is that most parents are very protective. They are helicopter or snowplow parents. They do not want their kids to fail or feel pain. They want their kids to get straight A's in school. They want their kids to be the best in sports, in the best clubs, and to be the best at everything, and failing is not an option. That is the worst phrase ever to utter to a child. And if they never fail as children, how will they deal with failure as adults? They've had no practice learning from failure.

One of the most heinous blunders in our world today is not talking about business at the dinner table. I hear story after story from young entrepreneurs who come from entrepreneurial families of how mom and dad would not talk about the family business or even let them work in it. The parents believed that their child should go off and do something different. They wanted them to have a better life. Well, tell me, what could be better than following the family history by taking over the business or by starting their own business with the knowledge and support of their family? A majority of the young people I work with want to be around their families.

In this day and age, entrepreneurs can no longer take the risks they used to be able to take 40 or 50 years ago. They have to have guidance, training, and mentorship to bring out their entrepreneurial spirit. This used to be taught at home, now it is left to the school systems. The financial risk is too great not to give them the tools necessary to succeed. When people are born to be entrepreneurs, they need help. They need education. They need resources that are going to get them farther in their ventures. Most importantly, they need to have the personal characteristics required to be an entrepreneur.

Chapter 16

What to Expect When Working with a Business Coach

Whenever clients first contact me, I always set up an appointment to meet face to face. I very rarely do a spur of the moment coaching session because I like to know a little bit about the entrepreneurs in advance, including the type of businesses or the industries they are going into. That way if I have never heard of it, I have the opportunity to research that field a little bit. I like to look into the legal aspect of their business ideas and get an understanding of the potential competition, be it locally or online. The initial coaching that I do with anyone has to be face to face. I will drive to them if need be. I will use Skype or an electronic meeting system if that is the only option for the initial meeting. I need to see their faces, expressions, and movements as they explain what they want to do. It gives me the ability to look into the eyes, because, as we all know, the eyes are the windows to the soul. The eyes are going to show me the passion for what the clients are working on, thinking about, or planning. I firmly believe that if somebody is truly passionate about an idea, I can see it in body movement, in the face, and it is definitely visible in the eyes when he or she talks about it. When entrepreneurs are passionate about what they do, their eyes will sparkle. I see it in them. I can also tell when they are giving me half-truths. The eyes never lie.

When I became a business coach, a philosophy that I adopted was to never tell anyone that he or she had a bad idea. The reason why I decided this is because though an idea did not sound good to me, or sound like something that *I* would do, it was not *my* business. Another philosophy I adopted was to not tell people what they *had* to do. Now, of course, legally there are certain things people have to do. If they want to work with me, they have to operate legally. That is just a requirement. They need to protect themselves and their personal assets. They have to have a Tax-ID number or EIN. If they have a partner, they need to form a formal partnership or become an S-Corp, Limited Liability Corporation, or Limited Liability Partnership, something that gives them a formal business structure. And if their idea itself is illegal, then of course, it is a no go. They must also follow standard business practices such as a basic accounting structure. They have to pay their taxes. All those things are required. After that, regarding how they run their business and everything that goes along with that, I just make suggestions or recommendations. However, having an outside perspective of their business gives me an advantage. Many times I can see things they cannot.

If somebody comes to me with an idea that is not practical or one where I can see little potential for revenue, one thing that I do is lay out all of the challenges that they will have to face to make this dream a reality. When I take this approach, apparently I often come across rather blunt. Many times I have heard their story before or I want them to understand that there are a lot of things they have to do to make their plan a reality. For example, a potential client wanted to open a fresh fish market in downtown Lincoln, Nebraska. Not that his idea was impossible, it just tended to be much more challenging than if he lived next to a coast or a major international airport.

Any business goal is even more of a challenge when the person with the ideas has little or no money and no access to capital. There seems to be a trend lately centered on nonprofit organizations. Many people want to start nonprofits, specifically those that protect animals. I like animals and have an adopted cat myself, but starting an animal shelter is especially difficult because of local ordinances, space, the cost of food and medicine, and chasing the same dollar that several other non-profits are after.

I want to make sure they understand that the real world is not going to sugar coat anything for them. When they are running a business, their customers want satisfaction. When running a business, they have to provide the satisfaction that their customers want. They have to run one of the best businesses out there. So whenever I am tough or am told I am obnoxious, or arrogant, or in some cases that I am full of it, I cannot change that perception, but I can guarantee you that they heard what I said, and that is what important.

When clients talk about their business idea or entrepreneurial dreams, the best way for me to help them in a short amount of time is by asking question about them and their ideas. The coaching method I have created for the initial meeting is a question-based interview. I cannot get the feedback I need from a questionnaire or essay. Talking allows the entrepreneurs to express themselves. It also forces them to put their ideas and passions into words.

Getting to Know the Entrepreneur

My job is to understand what clients want to do and then understand how much they know about it. I try to uncover gaps in their knowledge of their field or industry, or in their financial history. I look for anything that will show me where

I can best fill in the missing information. I have formulated a list of questions that I use as a starting point for every interview.

25 Questions You Need to Ask Yourself

1. What type of business are you planning?
2. (Or) What type of product do you want to produce?
3. Why do you want to start this business or create this product?
4. What kind of experience do you have with this product or industry?
5. Is this product going to be your main source of revenue?
6. Who is going to buy your product?
7. How much are they going to pay for your product?
8. Where and how are they going to get your product?
9. Have you ever owned a business before?
10. If no, why do you want to do this now?
11. How far into the process are you?
    a. What stage of development is the product or service?
    b. Are there any licensing requirements or current patents for the product?
12. Do you have a business plan?
    a. If they do not, I briefly explain the benefits of a business plan.
13. Where do you want to launch your business?
14. How many other companies do what you do?
    a. What sets you apart or will set you apart from other companies?
    b. What can the others do that you cannot?
15. Have you looked into funding?
    a. If yes, what kinds of funding have you looked into?
    b. Do you have an established banking relationship?
16. How much do you personally plan to invest in the business?
17. What are your goals for the company and for you as a business owner?
18. How much time are you planning to devote to the venture?
19. Do you have any mentors?
20. Have you sought legal advice?
21. Do you have an insurance agent?

22. Are you going to need an accountant or bookkeeper or can you do your own books?
23. Do you know how to register your business name and obtain a Tax ID number?
24. Who knows you are getting ready to start this venture?
25. What does your family say about all of this?

If they are a current business owner, the questions are a little different and are usually shaped by their responses. I always ask about their business: name, location, products, and any pertinent information they would like to give me. Then I ask why they wanted to come see me. The reason is not because things are going swimmingly! If I cannot get them to open up about their situation, then I ask them to tell me about their last week, something that will give a little insight as to what's going on. If that does not work, then I will ask a personal question: "How are you doing?" I want to see what their mental state is like and to understand their thought processes. Are stressed or are they truly enjoying everything that they are doing? I often get an exasperated sigh as an answer. That sigh speaks volumes. Even if I do get an "Everything's fine" type of answer, their eyes are a dead give-away. However, more often than not, they are more than willing to talk about their problems. They are so relieved that someone will listen to them and hopefully provide some solutions to their problems.

As a coach, it is my job to get to the bottom of everything. I need to find out whether they are really doing well or, if they aren't, to discover why. With clients who have an idea and are just starting to develop it, I ask them what obstacles they have uncovered. Some of the challenges they are facing are not in their businesses, but in their personal lives. Most people are working full time and are not able to break away from that job until the new business actually starts generating significant revenue. That is a huge challenge that we have to work through during the coaching sessions. It can be a delicate balance act of maintaining current employment while building a business that will eventually create their financial stability.

If they are currently in business, I will ask what business challenges they are having. Are they financial, marketing and sales, or employee issues? The goal is to uncover the biggest issues they are facing at that moment. Sometimes this is not easy. Many times the issues they believe are the biggest really are not. Most of the time the real challenges surface later in the conversation. Sometimes they are testing me as a coach to see whether I really know what I am doing, but generally it is a trust issue. Once I have gained their trust, then I will truly see all the challenges that they are facing.

The Right Solution for the Right Problem

Because entrepreneurs are so busy dealing with all of the hustle and bustle of their businesses, occasionally they encounter problems that need to be fixed. They look at the problem that is before them and believe they have to come up with a solution to fix it. What they sometimes fail to do is look at all of the factors leading up to the discovery of the issue. If the problem is the inability to track inventory, the first thing that pops into their heads is the need for funding to buy software that can do the job for them. What they really need to do is figure out why there is a problem with the current inventory system.

Once a young lady named Lori came to see me. The very first thing that she said after I asked her how things were going was, "Everything is fine." It was abrupt, but nothing too alarming. I asked her to tell me about her business. She owned a retail clothing store catering to the hip-hop crowd. Lori then told me that she had a part-time employee, Jack. Everything with him was "good." Traffic to the store was constant. She was financially OK. She was even buying inventory on a regular basis. I asked her why she was coming to talk to me if everything was in her words "fine." She finally told me that there seemed to be a problem with her inventory control. She was having difficulty figuring out what was in the store and when it was being sold. In my mind, the simple solution would be to invest in a new cash register with a point-of-sale system and inventory control software. This would require some capital outlay, but if she was bringing in regular revenue, this should not be a problem. We talked about this as a possible solution to her problem. She agreed it could work and went off to figure out how to pay for such a system.

It took two more meetings to discover that Lori had absolutely no record keeping system whatsoever. Everything was written down on paper if she and Jack remembered to write it down. She had a cash register that was only being used for holding cash. Jack worked evenings and was giving discounts on inventory and not writing them down. She didn't know about the discounts until she was approached by one of his regular customers demanding Jack's usual discount. On the flip-side, she was also giving discounts on inventory to people whom she thought would not pay full price. Inevitably, word got around that she would "discount" anything.

On top of all that, she had no idea how much inventory was in her back room. She had inventory from three years ago, as we discovered, and in the clothing world, that's not a good thing. The fourth meeting uncovered another issue that actually put the business in jeopardy. She had a business partner who had passed away within the last year. That complicated everything because the business was included in the will, and therefore, half of the business belonged to his estate, which could then be split among his family and relatives.

Because there was a legal issue, I insisted she contact a lawyer and an accountant to help get her affairs in order. Luckily, upon further investigation, her partner's half of the store was actually willed to her. With that part resolved, the accountant discovered the cash register she already could keep track of inventory. She just had to design a system for labeling her clothes and have it programmed into the register. After a talk with her employee, Lori decided he needed to find employment elsewhere.

She hired a college student majoring in business to take the evening shift and to help with marketing. There were no more discounts unless items were on sale or out of season. The last time I spoke with her it was good seeing a sparkle in her eyes instead of fear. She recently sold the store to another entrepreneur in the neighborhood who was looking to expand.

This case was a bit unusual. Generally, the major issue causing the entrepreneur grief is exposed in the first few minutes of conversation. Lori's issues were layered and slowly discovered. What started as an inventory control question led to the discovery of some major legal and accounting problems. Entrepreneurs have to trust somebody to tell the whole story. They will sometimes only give half the story when they're not completely comfortable or when they are hiding the real problem. This mutual commitment will help discover all of the issues and craft the proper resolutions.

Bright Ideas and Big Dreams

As your business grows, hopefully you'll have new ideas you want to try and maybe even some big dreams for where your company will go and what it will do. One thing you will need to do as an entrepreneur is do a reality check. If you do not have the ability to do this on your own, then seek out a business. I know they will have no problem becoming your "Mr. or Ms. Reality."

Many times, entrepreneurs have dreams about what their business can be, and that is great. The thing is, they have to find out what is real. There is a very big difference between dreams and reality. As a business coach, it is my job to help bring reality to the entrepreneur for that dream. My job is, as some put it, to punch holes in the new ideas they bring to me. I bring up as many issues I can see with their idea, both good and bad. I try to come up with all of the roadblocks I know they may encounter, generally things they have not thought of such as legalities or local ordinances that will stand in their way. Sometimes it is simply the fact that the product line that they are suggesting does not fit their mission. Maybe the technology that they want either does not exist or they do not have access to it. Sometimes it seems as if the dream is that—just a pipe dream.

My job is not to tell them that they cannot do it. It is to make sure they understand what is going to be involved if they decide to go down that path. Many times, when I start bringing reality to the dream, they come to the understanding that it really is just a dream. Or maybe it is an idea that could be saved for a later date, but it should not be enacted right now because it does not really fit their current business strategies, or they do not have the money to do it. Being a dream smasher is not a bad thing—I have to be able to do that as a business coach to help people.

My job is to provide enlightenment—a reality check. Their job is to assess the information given and determine whether they can modify what they want to do and make it fit now or within the nearest timeframe. It is their job to take the information, to take the criticism, the critiques, and say, "How can I use this information and make it work for me?" This process will utilize their talents, education, and experiences to make realistic decisions.

Whenever a restaurant owner client calls me, he starts off the conversation by saying, "I need you to talk me off the ledge." He knows he is about to make a decision that could potentially make his business take a plunge. He will then go on to explain his predicament. And we talk it out. The first couple of time I received that phone call it was as bad as he thought it was. But as time went on and he grew as an entrepreneur, his "ledge" moments became less and less because he learned to recognize what could be and what was just a dream.

Entrepreneurs need to dream, and they need to be creative because one of the things about being in business is that they have to be able to see the future. They probably do not need a crystal ball, but if in an industry long enough, they should be able to predict what will happen in the future based on what is going on now and what has happened in the past. They should read industry magazines, attend conferences, and network with competitors to help with this predicting. These activities are necessary if they want to stay current or bring new products to their customers. They want to make sure they have everything their clients need right now, but they also need to be thinking about what the customer will need tomorrow.

The other thing that entrepreneurs need to do once they have seen their future is plan for it. If they do not create a way to get to the future, then the vision will probably go away or get lost in the traffic of day-to-day business. The planning process will help determine the fiscal requirement for this new future. Is there going to be a new product line, more employees, or a new facility? Business owners have to be able to plan for this and write it out. Funders will want to see this written plan. If the entrepreneur is smart, if they understand what is going on, and if they look to the future and plan for it, the path for success is a whole lot smoother.

Before you plunge forward with a new idea or a big dream, ask yourself:

- Does this fit with my current mission? Or am I really thinking about a different business? (Do I really want to start another business?)
- Will this change confuse my current customers?
- Will have to go get a new set of customers?
- Will I need new marketing? How much? How much will that cost?
- Will I need new employees or more space? How much will that cost and will I generate enough revenue to re-coup those costs?
- Are there laws, licenses, or zoning issues to consider?
- What is the cost of the technology I will need? How long will it take the investment in that technology to pay for itself?
- Does this fit with the trends in my industry? Is it too far ahead, for example, using expensive and untested technology? Or too far behind, for example, capitalizing on a fad that is fading? You don't have to follow trends—sometimes huge opportunities come from not doing what everyone else is doing. But think twice about it because you have to be very careful and very strategic.
- Does this work toward my big, long-term business goals? Or is it a distraction?

The Big Picture

If you don't have a coach, one thing you're going to have to do for yourself is remember to celebrate your successes. It is very important that entrepreneurs tell all the successes that they have had in their business, every success that they have had in researching it, everything that makes them feel good about what they are doing or what they want to do. I use this information to help them realize that even though there are tough times starting a business, they can look back at all of the good things that have happened. I tell them to write down their successes. They should keep the list handy and add to it frequently because entrepreneurs tend to focus on the negative and the list will show them they are doing well. It is a necessity to point out the positive in what they have done. In the notes I keep, I make sure to jot down the successes I know and hear about because I know I am going to have to go back to those successes and remind them what they have done and what they should be proud of.

Chapter 17

An Entrepreneur Is Never Alone

Starting a business is fun. It is also exciting, scary, expensive, risky, and not something that everyone can do. The entrepreneurial spirit is an asset that a select few possess. It is what some few people thrive on. These rare spirits can take advantage of an opportunity and make it work for them. I love that about entrepreneurs. I love working with these people, helping them figure out their directions in life, and watching them grow. It's tough to see them when they are struggling, going through growing pains, bad times, bad employees, funding issues, and scraping to make ends meet. But it is still a pleasure to work with them because they do not give up. They may get down, but they always try to figure out how to go on to the next step. That is the exhilarating part. That is the part that makes working with an entrepreneur exciting.

What entrepreneurs cannot forget is that they do not have to go it alone. There are people out there who want to help them like business coaches and mentors. Resources organizations that are geared specifically for their needs are available. One of the big things that they have to learn to do is ask for help. Just talking to somebody from time to time is usually enough to get them going to the next level. But if they run from their problems, they will end up running from everyone and everything which will end up being bad for their business. Whenever there is an issue, entrepreneurs need to be less like an island and more like a community.

Business coaches are there for that reason. Even if a business coach is not available, there are several other organizations that can help. Local chambers of commerce, community colleges, and state economic development departments often have people who are available to talk to business owners or future business owners. Entrepreneurs really need to take the time to ask questions and tell their stories.

Thriving businesses don't just benefit their owners. They are crucial for the economy on all levels, local, state, and national. Entrepreneurs bring businesses to our communities. They fill empty buildings on Main Street and employ local citizens. Our country was built on the premise of entrepreneurship—people making a life for themselves and for their families. The entrepreneurial spirit is alive and well. If it resides in you, you are one of the lucky ones. Now is the best time to explore any business idea you have been pondering. Now is the time to become the entrepreneur you always wanted to be.

Afterword

I Don't Remember Becoming a Dad

As a coach, I sometimes get to work with businesses from their very beginnings as a business owner. It is fascinating to watch the entrepreneur change and grow from the beginning of the process to end. I get to be a little part of all that. It is a privilege to see them evolve as a person and grow their business into something that is sustainable in the outside world. Watching the whole thing is a phenomenal experience. It is one of the best things that I have ever done in my many years in the business world. They do all the work, and I just get to stand back and sometimes get to say, "You're doing good." It's a lot like being a dad. I get to see them become someone they themselves can be proud of. And just like a dad, it's hard watching them make mistakes. It is difficult, but watching them pick themselves back up and go on to do something that they never even thought that they could do is the best thing. Offering genuine praise to an entrepreneur is not a difficult thing because it really does a heart good to watch them go through the processes that they are going through and become someone in this world. It's a good thing.

Entrepreneurs like to show rough exteriors, but I have had several crying in my office. Not because I have said nasty things to them, but because they are very happy, are going through a tough time, or are very tired. Tears flow freely with entrepreneurs, and that has to do with the passion and the emotion of everything that they are doing. Having all of that bottled up inside, and then having somebody to talk to about it is a great thing for them. A coach means being there for the tears and to give them the hugs when they need it. It means to be there as a friend if they need it, but also to be the person who says, "No, that is not a good idea," or "Maybe you should look into that harder before you go down that road." They need that somebody who can be the caution light for them and who can present all of the issues yet encourage them to go forward. That is one of the great things about being a coach, especially when they come with these harebrained ideas that you know are going to mess up their business. They are not thinking properly; they have not had enough sleep or are not eating properly or something.

All entrepreneurs need help in some form or another and that is what a coach does. Business owners like to think they can do it all. However, I have seen these strong people who "can do it all" in my office, pulling their hair out, and mad about whatever happened to them that day. What I have found is that their breakdown of sorts often revolves around their stubborn refusal to admit that they're wrong or that they need help. If they would just ask for help, if they would just figure out a plan for help, or if they would create a system for help, it would make their lives so much better.

When a business coach can provide good solid advice and options that leads to successes, they become a trusted resource for their entrepreneurs. Part of being a business coach is that when you gain entrepreneurs' trust, they start coming to you to discuss all matters of their lives. The topics can range from child issues, personal finances, past indiscretions, encounters with the law, marriage problems, dating advice, coming out of the closet, and drug and alcohol use, just to name a few. It does not matter how personal it is; if the trust is there, they will talk about it.

Coaching has great rewards, but comes with great challenges. To be effective, entrepreneurs have to be open to coaching and they have to listen. They do not have to take all of the advice, but coaches are people who stand outside of the businesses and look in. Many times their perspective is a bit different and can lead to outcomes that can be extremely beneficial to the entrepreneur.